A VISUAL ENCYCLOPEDIA OF MODERN

AMERICAN PRESIDENTS

FROM THEODORE ROOSEVELT
TO BARACK OBAMA

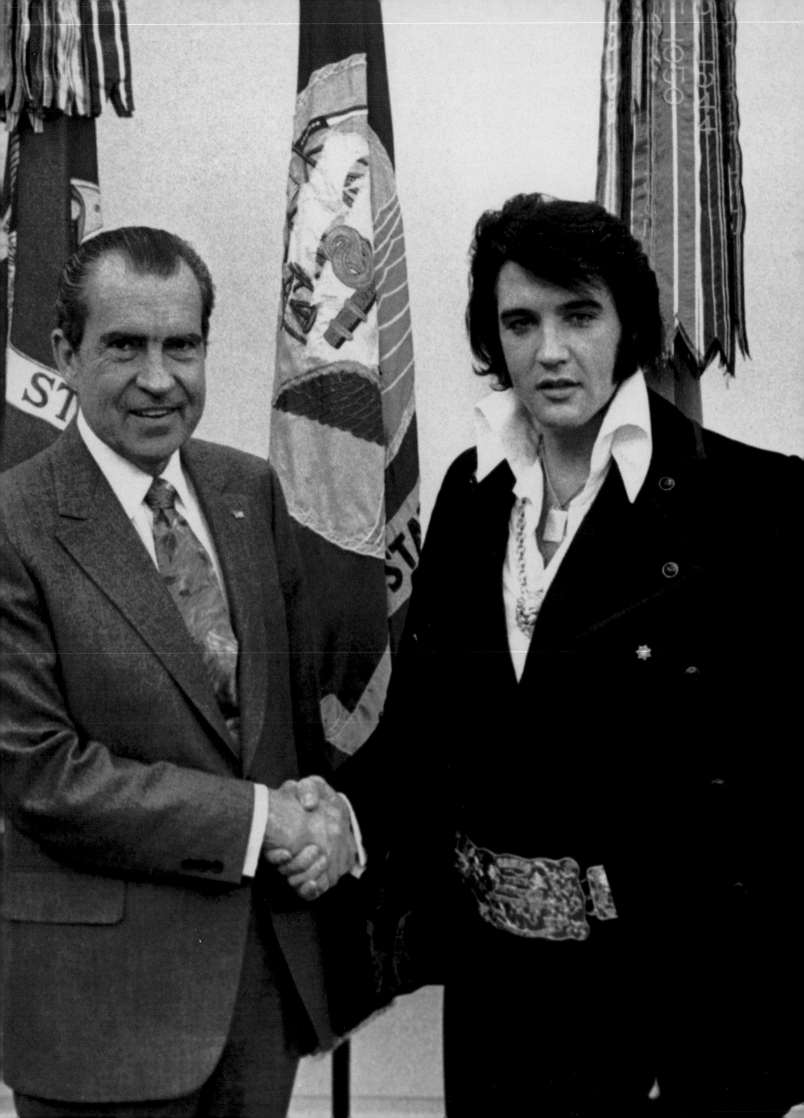

A VISUAL ENCYCLOPEDIA OF MODERN

AMERICAN PRESIDENTS

FROM THEODORE ROOSEVELT TO BARACK OBAMA

PROFESSOR JON ROPER

southwater

This edition is published by Southwater
an imprint of Anness Publishing Ltd
Blaby Road, Wigston
Leicestershire LE18 4SE
Email: info@anness.com

Web: www.southwaterbooks.com;
www.annesspublishing.com

Anness Publishing has a new picture agency outlet for
images for publishing, promotions or advertising.
Please visit our website www.practicalpictures.com for
more information.

Publisher: Joanna Lorenz
Editorial Director: Helen Sudell
Project Editor: Simona Hill
Designer: Nigel Partridge
All state flags illustrated by Alfred Znamierowski
All maps illustrated by Tom Connell
Production Controller: Christine Ni

ETHICAL TRADING POLICY
Because of our ongoing ecological investment
programme, you, as our customer, can have the
pleasure and reassurance of knowing that a tree is
being cultivated on your behalf to naturally replace
the materials used to make the book you are holding.
For further information about this scheme, go to
www.annesspublishing.com/trees

CONTENTS

INTRODUCTION

The president of the USA is the world's most powerful political leader, a fact that George Washington, the country's first president, could never have envisaged when he took office more than 200 years ago. Washington is ranked as one of the greatest presidents to have served his country, but few of his successors have soared to such iconic stature.

Beginning in 1901, this chronological guide to the presidents of the 20th and early 21st centuries provides an overview of the calibre of politicians elected to high office. Each is set within the context of major social and economic challenges and advances that have influenced and shaped domestic affairs, as well as the course of international relations.

Among the 19 presidents elected since 1901, only Theodore Roosevelt, Woodrow Wilson and Franklin Roosevelt have, so far, established historical reputations that match the most distinguished of their predecessors, including George Washington, Thomas Jefferson and Abraham Lincoln.

Between 1904 and 1932, Republicans won five out of seven presidential elections: Theodore Roosevelt served out William McKinley's second term, following McKinley's assassination in 1901, before winning the popular vote in his own right. William Taft and Herbert Hoover were one-term presidents and Calvin Coolidge inherited the presidency from Warren Harding, the first 20th-century chief executive to die from natural causes while in office.

Below: The carvings on Mount Rushmore have immortalized four presidents, only one of which, Theodore Roosevelt, came to power in the 20th century.

PRESIDENTIAL ROLL CALL

Theodore Roosevelt, 1901–1909
William Taft, 1909–1913
Woodrow Wilson, 1913–1921
Warren Harding, 1921–1923
Calvin Coolidge, 1923–1929
Herbert Hoover, 1929–1933
Franklin Roosevelt, 1933–1945
Harry Truman, 1945–1953
Dwight Eisenhower, 1953–1961
John F. Kennedy, 1961–1963
Lyndon B. Johnson, 1963–1969
Richard Nixon, 1969–1974
Gerald Ford, 1974–1977
Jimmy Carter, 1977–1981
Ronald Reagan, 1981–1989
George H. W. Bush, 1989–1993
Bill Clinton, 1993–2001
George W. Bush, 2001–2009
Barack Obama, 2009–

Above: Uncle Sam, who personifies the government of the USA.

Modern politics begins in 1934 with the election of Franklin D. Roosevelt. His unique achievement was not only his longevity in office (he occupied the White House for just over 12 years); he was also the architect of the modern presidency. Yet Roosevelt's example created the paradox of contemporary presidential power: while its potential has increased, his successors have struggled to use it successfully. His legacy has yet to be surpassed.

Since Franklin Roosevelt won his four consecutive elections, Democrats have not enjoyed much greater success than they had before he entered the White House: in the 15 presidential contests held since 1948, when Harry Truman achieved an upset and an unanticipated victory, they have won on only six occasions.

Like Truman, Lyndon Johnson inherited the White House following the death of his predecessor (John F. Kennedy) and was then elected in his own right. His presidency was another political watershed: he was the first chief executive from a former Confederate state to win election. Four of the eight presidents elected after Johnson have come from the South: Jimmy Carter from Georgia, Bill Clinton from Arkansas, the Texas-based George H.W. Bush and most recently his eldest son. Indeed, George W. Bush was the first member of Abraham Lincoln's party raised in the former Confederacy to become president of the United States of America.

Eight of those elected since 1900 have been former state governors. Seven, including Gerald Ford who was appointed to the office and who inherited the presidency on Richard Nixon's resignation, were former vice presidents. Six had served in the Senate. Three – William Taft, Herbert Hoover and Dwight Eisenhower – had not held elected office prior to entering the White House.

John F. Kennedy was assassinated, and Ronald Reagan narrowly survived an attempt on his life. The president's security has become a perennial problem and a paramount concern.

While some may be tempted to cut themselves off from their fellow citizens, contact between politicians and voters remains the air that breathes life into American democracy. Nowhere is this better demonstrated than in the small towns of states such as Iowa and New Hampshire as the nominating process begins anew every four years and aspirants to the office meet potential supporters of their cause.

Above: Barack Obama, the first black president of the USA.

The presidency combines constitutional authority and political power. Over the past 200 years it has become the most important institution of America's federal government and is at the centre of national political life. In the 21st century, who may join Wilson, the Roosevelts, Jefferson, Lincoln and Washington as an authoritative and revered president who provides the USA with a lasting legacy for the collective good?

Left and below: The Republican party symbol is the elephant, while that of the Democratic party is the donkey.

CHAPTER ONE

THEODORE ROOSEVELT TO WOODROW WILSON

1901–1921

THEODORE ROOSEVELT LIKED THE IDEA OF US IMPERIALISM. WILLIAM TAFT HAD BEEN AN ADMINISTRATOR IN PART OF ITS EMPIRE. WOODROW WILSON BELIEVED IN THE IMPERIALISM OF AN IDEA: DEMOCRACY. FOR THE THREE PRESIDENTS ELECTED BETWEEN 1904 AND 1920, IT WAS A TIME OF DOMESTIC POLITICAL TURBULENCE, WITH THE DEMOCRATS PROFITING FROM DIVISIONS IN THE REPUBLICAN PARTY TO WIN BACK THE WHITE HOUSE FOR THE FIRST TIME IN 16 YEARS. THE EARLY 20TH CENTURY WAS THE AGE OF PROGRESSIVISM, BRINGING GOVERNMENT'S POWER TO BEAR IN THE STILL LARGELY UNREGULATED WORLD OF US CAPITALISM. IT WAS ALSO A PERIOD OF INTERNATIONAL TENSIONS, CULMINATING IN EUROPEAN EMPIRES FIGHTING WORLD WAR I: THE 'WAR TO END ALL WARS'. THE LEAGUE OF NATIONS, THE AMERICAN PRESIDENT'S LAST BEST HOPE FOR A FUTURE WITHOUT GLOBAL CONFLICT, FAILED TO KEEP WHAT PROVED TO BE A FRAGILE PEACE.

Left: The Great White Fleet was a demonstration of the USA's naval power and the country's arrival on the world stage.

THEODORE ROOSEVELT

1901–1909

Republican bosses thought Theodore Roosevelt was a maverick, appropriately enough for a one-time rancher out West, and conspired to place him where he could not do much political damage: the vice presidency. An anarchist's bullet then put him in the White House. In 1904 he defied tradition, becoming the first president who had inherited the office to be elected to it in his own right. He did not run for re-election in 1908 and during the administration of his successor, William Taft, he spent four years regretting his public commitment only to serve one full term. So in 1912 he ran again as the candidate of his own

Below: Roosevelt's was a high-energy presidency. Aged 42, he was the youngest president to take office.

Progressive party. He came second. Theodore Roosevelt was an elemental and unquenchable political force, whose impact upon the United States and the presidency was profound.

EARLY LIFE

Born in 1858, into a wealthy New York family, he was named for his father, a prominent businessman. The elder Theodore supported Lincoln during the Civil War, avoiding active service because Roosevelt's mother, Martha, came from a slave-owning family in Georgia and had relatives fighting for the Confederacy.

Roosevelt Jr was asthmatic, and as a teenager he worked to overcome his illness through a programme of rigorous physical exercise. It was an early

Born: 27 October 1858, New York, New York
Parents: Theodore (1831–78) and Martha (1834–84)
Family background: Business
Education: Harvard College (1880)
Religion: Dutch Reformed
Occupation: Author, public official
Military service: Colonel, US army, Spanish–American War
Political career: New York State Assembly, 1882–4
Civil Service Commision, 1889–95
Assistant secretary of the navy, 1897–8
Governor of New York, 1898–1900
Vice president, 1901
Presidential annual salary: $50,000
Political party: Republican
Died: 6 January 1919, Oyster Bay, New York

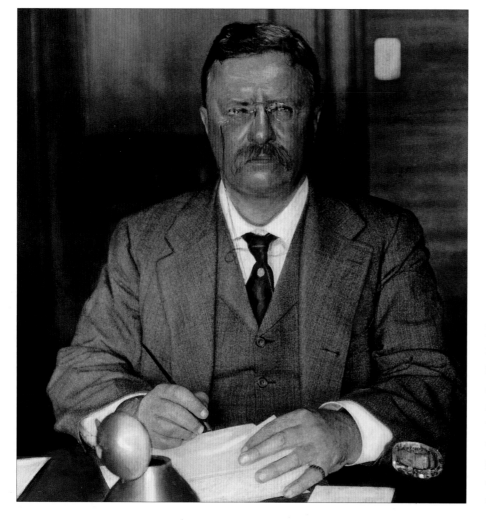

example of his self-discipline and obsession with what he called "the strenuous life". In 1876, he entered Harvard and beside academic pursuits took up wrestling and boxing. While he was there, in 1878, his father died. Roosevelt married Alice Hathaway Lee in 1880, the year he graduated. Two years later he dropped out of Columbia Law School to begin the first of two terms in the New York State Assembly as its youngest elected member.

His private life and a career in public service seemed settled, but on Valentine's Day 1884, it all fell apart. Roosevelt's mother died from typhoid fever and a few hours later his wife succumbed to a fatal kidney infection, dying in his arms. His diary entry for that day, written under a large cross, was devastatingly simple: "The light has gone out of my life." His first child, a daughter named Alice, was just two days old.

Leaving Alice with his sister, Roosevelt spent the next two years in the Badlands of Dakota, ranching, hunting and laying down the law as a local deputy sheriff. On his return to the city, in November 1886, he campaigned unsuccessfully to become mayor of New York. A month later, in London, he married his second wife, Edith Carow.

At home in Oyster Bay, New York, Roosevelt resumed a writing career that had started with the publication of his first book, *The Naval War of 1812* in 1882, publishing among other works the first volume of *The Winning of the West* (1889), a romanticized version of the USA's expansion across the continent. In 1897, following appointments to the United States Civil Service Commission and as president of the New York City Police Commission, he became assistant secretary of the navy in President McKinley's administration. He resigned to fight in the Spanish–American War.

Elected governor of New York, in November 1898, he rapidly became a nuisance to the party. His mistake, in the eyes of the state's Republican bosses, was to support taxes on the public utility companies, which were important donors to the party machine. The Republican leader in New York, Thomas Platt, consulted with Mark Hanna, President McKinley's influential political adviser, and Roosevelt was manoeuvred into reluctantly accepting the vice-presidential nomination for the 1900 election. Nobody anticipated the assassination that would make "that damned cowboy", as Hanna dismissively called him, the youngest president to assume the office. On 14 September 1901, Theodore Roosevelt became chief executive at the age of 42.

A NEW CENTURY

When Roosevelt came to the White House in 1901, the United States had taken its place among the most industrialized nations of the age, and he aimed to demonstrate its potential to wield an unprecedented influence in world affairs. His energies were now focused on his ambition: an administration of unparalleled achievement. It was a compelling performance. Roosevelt

Above: Roosevelt's charge with the 'Rough Riders' (a volunteer regiment) up San Juan Hill in Cuba, carrying a revolver salvaged from the US battleship Maine*, was the stuff of heroic legend. The action was pivotal in propelling him to elective office as governor of New York in 1898.*

knew the political value of dramatic gestures: just over a month after taking office he invited Booker T. Washington, the prominent black civil rights activist, to the White House for dinner. He appreciated the persuasive power of what he called the "bully pulpit" of the presidency. He courted the press, and had the priceless talent of providing them with a memorable quote, the pre-radio equivalent of a sound bite. "Speak softly and carry a big stick" not only described his foreign policy, but also provided a gift for commentators and newspaper cartoonists.

THE PANAMA CANAL

During 1901 the USA and Britain negotiated a treaty opening the way for the construction of a canal across the

Central American isthmus. There were two possible routes to link the Atlantic and Pacific Oceans: through Nicaragua or Panama. Roosevelt backed the second option. After some complex financial, political and diplomatic manoeuvrings, together with a judicious US naval blockade to establish Panama as an independent republic, in 1904 work began.

TRUST-BUSTING

In February 1902, President Roosevelt announced that the federal government would prosecute the Northern Securities Company for violations of

EDITH ROOSEVELT

Born in Connecticut in 1861 and a childhood friend of Roosevelt's sister Corrine, Edith Carow was a teenager when he proposed marriage: she refused. A year after his first wife died, he asked again and she accepted. Edith raised her stepdaughter, Alice, and five children of her own. As first lady, she supervised the White House's restoration, organizing it to reconcile the competing demands of public and family life. She died in 1948 aged 87.

Right: The French first tried building the Panama Canal. After the loss of 22,000 lives, they gave up.

Left: Constructing the Panama Canal, connecting two oceans, was one of the most difficult engineering tasks ever undertaken.

the Sherman Anti-Trust Act (which aimed to curb the activities of cartels and monopolies), taking on the world's leading banker, John Pierpont Morgan, one of the 20 or so financiers and industrialists who controlled the US economy. The *Detroit Free Press* observed, "Wall Street is paralyzed at the thought that a President of the United States should sink so low as to enforce the law." Two years later, by a one-vote majority, the Supreme Court ruled that Northern Securities should be broken up. Roosevelt's 'trust-busting' – more cases followed – gained him widespread popular support. In all, 44 lawsuits were initiated against major US corporations.

CONSERVATION

Roosevelt's abiding interest in the natural world and the memories of his experiences living on the US frontier combined in his commitment to conservation. In May 1902, he signed the bill establishing Crater Lake in Oregon as a National Park, the first of the five that he would create while president. Unpopular with business interests at the

time, his policy of bringing the USA's wilderness lands under public protection, and preventing their destruction through the exploitation of natural resources, proved to be of immeasurable benefit to future generations.

THE SQUARE DEAL

In 1902, hoping to use the persuasive powers of the presidency to end a coal strike in Pennsylvania that threatened the nation's heating supplies, Roosevelt met mine owners and union leaders at the White House. Negotiations stalled. The president threatened to use a big stick domestically: he suggested that federal troops could be used to take over the mines, which would then be run by the government. The negotiations were resumed, and both sides accepted arbitration. Roosevelt called it a "Square Deal" and coined the slogan for his 1904 election campaign. Surfing a wave of popular support, he won easily, admitting himself "glad to be elected President in my own right".

SECOND ADMINISTRATION

Before he took the oath of office for a second time, in December 1904, he announced the 'Roosevelt Corollary' to the Monroe Doctrine (which had been announced in 1823 and asserted

that the United States had a sphere of influence that included its neighbours to the south). Under Roosevelt's amendment, the United States assumed the right "to the exercise of an international police power" in Latin America. This more interventionist policy towards its neighbours provoked increasing resentment at 'Yankee Imperialism' but reflected what Roosevelt saw as the USA's necessary involvement in what was widely regarded as its backyard.

Below: Crater lake lies in a volcanic basin in Oregon. It was protected by legislation brought in by Roosevelt.

Left: Slum-living in squalid, cramped conditions was a reality of life for many in the early years of the 20th century.

At home, the United States still needed cleaning up. Investigative journalists, whom Roosevelt characterized as "muckrakers", after the character in *Pilgrim's Progress* "who could look no way but downward, with a muckrake in his hand", highlighted the unsafe industrial practices and squalor that prompted the progressive politics of the period. In 1906, the president read the scathing exposure of corruption in Upton Sinclair's book, *The Jungle*, which portrayed with grim accuracy the sickening malpractices of the meat-packing factories. With public approval the president approved the first legislation regulating the industry, paving the way for the creation of the Food and Drug Administration. It was among the last of his significant domestic reforms.

In 1905, he used personal diplomacy to end the war that had broken out between Russia and Japan the previous year, mediating peace talks in New Hampshire. His efforts were recognized with the 1906 Nobel Peace Prize: the first time it had been awarded to a recipient outside Europe. The following year, Roosevelt sent the US fleet,

STATES ENTERING THE UNION DURING ROOSEVELT'S PRESIDENCY: OKLAHOMA

Entered the Union: 1907
Pre-state history: Indian Territory (1856) ceded land to US after Civil War; opened for settlement by land rush (1889)
Total population in 1910 census: 1,657,155
Electoral College votes in 1908: 7

painted white for the occasion, on a voyage around the world. It symbolized the USA's sea power: only the British navy was now superior in size.

Roosevelt left the White House in 1909, at the age of 50. He had explored the possibilities of presidential power and made the office the focus of national attention in a manner unrivalled since the Civil War.

AFTER THE PRESIDENCY

Declaring himself "as fit as a Bull Moose", the popular name given to his insurgent political party, Roosevelt returned to the political arena in the presidential election of 1912. He split the Republican vote. Woodrow Wilson won. After that, he was a spent political force. He wrote, travelled, and when the United States entered World War I, volunteered to be part of the action. The government refused his offer. In 1919, Theodore Roosevelt's remarkable life ended: he died in his sleep on 6 January. According to *The New York Times* his last words were to his black servant: "Please put out that light, James."

THE INVENTION OF FLIGHT
THE WRIGHT BROTHERS

On 17 December 1903, after a first attempt at flight had ended when his elder brother Wilbur stalled on take-off, Orville Wright flew a powered heavier-than-air machine above an isolated beach at Kitty Hawk, North Carolina. The flight lasted 12 seconds. Wilbur tried again: another 12-second flight. The third flight, Orville's turn, was three seconds longer. Finally, Wilbur managed almost a minute in the air, travelling about 1km (more than half a mile) and landing before a gust of wind destroyed the brothers' successful prototype.

Orville sent a telegram to his father: "Success four flights Thursday morning … started from level with engine power alone … longest 57 seconds inform Press home Christmas." Laconic words, an eye for publicity and a dash of domesticity described the historic achievement: the Wright brothers had invented an aeroplane.

Having mastered the technology of flight, the Wright brothers tried to capitalize on their inventive genius. From the outset, they believed that the military would be interested in aeroplanes. In January 1905, they approached the US War Department. A letter outlined their previous year's achievements, linking one of them with President Roosevelt's election success:

Above: In 1904 the Wright brothers were able to fly a complete circle, and stay in the air for more than five minutes.

"The first of these record flights was made on November 9th, in celebration of the phenomenal political victory of the preceding day, and the second on December 1st, in honour of the one hundredth flight of the season."

The government remained unconvinced. Three years later, after the brothers had tried to interest Europeans by exhibiting their aeroplane in a number of countries, the Roosevelt administration finally invited tenders for a contract to supply a machine. In September 1906, Orville made a series of demonstration flights at Fort Myers, Virginia, witnessed by spectators including Theodore Roosevelt Jr. The following year, the army bought the Wright brothers' aeroplane.

Wilbur died in 1912, but Orville lived until 1948, through the two World Wars in which air power became increasingly important. Air warfare would claim the life of President Roosevelt's youngest and favourite son, Quentin, who joined the US Army Air Corps and was shot down over France in July 1918.

Below: The Wright brothers' first flight covered less distance than the wingspan of a Boeing 747 jet.

THE SAN FRANCISCO EARTHQUAKE

1906

"Hear rumors of great disaster through an earthquake in San Francisco but know nothing, or the real facts. Call upon me for any assistance I can render." The telegram to the governor of California, George Pardee, came from President Roosevelt. San Francisco had

Below: To restore business confidence the extent of the damage to the area was played down.

always been vulnerable. At just after 5 a.m. on Wednesday 18 April 1906, the earthquake struck. Chinatown was obliterated. Countless buildings collapsed. Fires raged and by Saturday morning, the city was a scrap yard. Even though news from the West Coast was sketchy, Roosevelt discussed the government's response with his Cabinet. Victor Metcalf, his secretary of commerce and a Californian, was sent to San Francisco to report back.

The president refused offers of foreign aid, but donations from other US cities and individuals including John D. Rockefeller and Andrew Carnegie were welcomed. Congress approved $2.5 million to support the relief efforts. Roosevelt, aware of the city's history of municipal corruption, announced on 22 April that funds would be channelled through the Red Cross, although subsequently he agreed that they should also go to the city's finance committee, set up as part of its co-ordinated response to the disaster.

Above: As the earth collapsed vertically and shifted horizontally along the San Andreas fault, San Francisco suffered one of the greatest urban catastrophes in American history. The fire ignited by the quake raged for three days.

On 26 April Metcalf sent the president a lengthy account of the damage done to the city and the progress of the relief effort: "It is almost impossible to describe the ruin wrought by the earthquake and especially the conflagration … The people however, are confident and hopeful for the future and have not in any sense lost their courage. They feel under deep obligations to you and the national Government for the prompt and efficient assistance rendered them."

The death toll was eventually estimated at more than 3,000. In 1915, the city hosted the Panama-Pacific International Exposition. Eighteen million visitors came to see the rebuilt metropolis on America's West Coast.

WILLIAM TAFT
1909–1913

William Taft achieved his lifetime's ambition after serving in an office in which he never felt at home. For many years his career was a reflection of the expectations and aspirations of others: his parents and his wife. His predecessor's inability to stay away from the political arena destroyed their friendship and wrecked the Republicans' prospects of winning a fifth consecutive presidential election. Unlike Theodore Roosevelt, William Taft later found that fulfilment and fresh horizons existed beyond the White House.

Taft was born in 1857 in the Republican stronghold of Ohio. His father went to Yale, became a lawyer, served as secretary of war in Grant's Cabinet and was briefly attorney general before spending time in Europe as a diplomat. Taft followed dutifully in

Born: 15 September 1857, Cincinnati, Ohio
Parents: Alphonso (1810–91) and Louisa (1827–1907)
Family background: Law and public service
Education: Yale College (1878); Cincinnati Law School (1880)
Religion: Unitarian
Occupation: Lawyer, public service
Military service: None
Political career: Ohio Superior Court judge, 1887–90
US solicitor general, 1890–2
US circuit court judge, 1892–1900
Governor of the Philippines, 1901–4
Secretary of war, 1904–8
US Supreme Court chief justice, 1921–30
Presidential annual salary: $75,000
Political party: Republican
Died: 8 March 1930, Washington DC

his father's footsteps, graduating from Yale in 1878 and embarking on a legal career. In 1886 he married Helen Herron, a judge's daughter. They had three children.

A superior court judge at the age of 30, Taft was appointed solicitor general by Benjamin Harrison. He hoped to become a Supreme Court justice. Instead President McKinley asked him

Above: Taft became president reluctantly – his lifetime's ambition was to be chief justice of the Supreme Court.

to govern the Philippines. He returned to Washington in 1904 as secretary of war, overseeing the construction of the Panama Canal and supervising the federal government's response to the San Francisco earthquake. His wife

HELEN TAFT

After visiting the White House as a teenager, Helen Herron aspired to become first lady. Born in Ohio in 1861, she married William Taft in 1886. Having achieved her life's ambition, in May 1909 she suffered a stroke. Her influential role in public life remained undiminished. She was 81 when she died in 1943.

STATES ENTERING THE UNION DURING TAFT'S PRESIDENCY:

NEW MEXICO

Entered the Union: 1912
Pre-state history: Land acquired after Mexican War (1848) added to as a result of 1850 Compromise; organized as Territory (1850) supplemented by Gadsden Purchase (1853)
Total population in 1920 census: 360,350
Electoral College votes in 1912: 3

ARIZONA

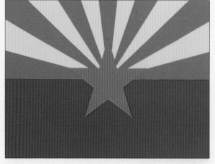

Entered the Union: 1912
Pre-state history: Land acquired through Gadsden Purchase (1853); part of Confederacy (1861); organized as Arizona Territory (1863)
Total population in 1920 census: 334,162
Electoral College votes in 1912: 3

wanted him to succeed Roosevelt, as did, initially, the president himself. Taft duly obtained the Republican nomination in the 1908 presidential election and easily defeated William Jennings Bryan, who was then making his third attempt to win the White House for the Democrats.

TARIFF REFORM

William Taft tackled an issue that Roosevelt, knowing its potential to cause political problems, had deftly avoided: his attempt at tariff reform antagonized Congress. But he proved a relentless 'trust-buster'. At this time much of the US economy was controlled by a system of trusts: virtual

Below: Taft tackled issues that his predecessor had chosen to ignore, and continued Roosevelt's trust-busting policy.

monopolies run by large groups of businesses. Taft ended many of them. He was a believer in the benefits of 'dollar diplomacy' – using the USA's economic power as leverage in international affairs, rather than displays of military might and imperial hubris – and his foreign policy promoted trade relations and sought to promote world peace.

He could never escape his predecessor's ambition, and it was this that sealed his fate in the 1912 election. After

leaving the White House, Taft taught at Yale Law School. In 1920 President Warren Harding gave him the job he had always really wanted: chief justice of the Supreme Court, a position he held until just before his death in 1930. He is the only president to have been chief justice.

Below: Taft forged ahead with 80 trust-busting suits, benefiting less well-off people, but alienating business leaders.

HENRY FORD AND THE MODEL 'T'
THE DEVELOPMENT OF THE MOTOR CAR

Not only did Henry Ford make a motor car that was affordable – changing it from an object of desire to an ordinary purchase – he also revolutionized industrial practices in the process. His innovation was a moving assembly line: by 1914, it took less than 100 minutes to make a Model 'T'. Rivals employed five times as many workers as did Henry Ford in order to construct their automobiles.

Mass production and low overheads were the key to increasing supply. Demand was created by another innovation. In 1914 the Ford Motor Company announced that it would pay its workers $5 an hour, more than double the minimum wage. This shocked his competitors, but for the workers it meant that working for Ford made it possible to buy one of his cars. High wages compensated for the drudgery of the work. Within two years Ford's company profits had doubled to

Below: The Model 'T' was the first cheaply available motor car, which was within the means and aspirations of many households.

$60 million and Henry Ford became rich while putting his fellow Americans behind the wheel of a car.

First launched in 1908, the Model 'T' sold for $850. It was reasonably reliable and easy to drive. The basic design of the 15 million that were made remained unchanged during its 19 years of production. Capable of reaching a speed of 30 miles an hour on a good road, of which there were then few, its versatile engine was useful for powering saws or grinding corn when its innovative steel alloy chassis was not transporting people and goods across the United States.

Ford became famous. He dabbled in politics, initially professing himself a Democrat, but revealing himself as an unreconstructed apostle of religious intolerance – he was accused of anti-semitism – and notoriously hostile to trade unions. His most quixotic political gesture came in 1915 when, having failed to persuade a sceptical President Wilson of his plan, he sponsored a 'Peace Ship' to Europe to try to stop World War I.

Above: Ford revolutionized the motor car industry, with the first assembly line production of vehicles.

Henry Ford's monument was the massive Rouge River factory in Detroit, where raw materials were moulded into rows of black Model 'T's. He was an industrial alchemist whose cars transformed American society.

Below: The 'peace ship' Oscar II, sponsored by Henry Ford, visited European nations to try to end the war.

THE NAACP

The 100th anniversary of Abraham Lincoln's birth fell on 12 February 1909. The date was marked by the first meeting of the National Association for the Advancement of Colored People (NAACP). The previous year, William Walling, who had strayed far from his family's roots as wealthy slave-owners in Kentucky, and had emerged from the University of Chicago as a committed socialist, had witnessed the brutality of the lynching and killing taking place during a riot in Lincoln's home town of Springfield, Illinois. Walling's description of these events, published in an article entitled *The Race War in the North*, ended with a plea for black equality, and posed the question: "Who realizes the seriousness of the situation, and what large and powerful body of citizens is ready to come to their aid?"

Mary White Ovington, a fellow socialist and civil rights campaigner, was one who answered the call. She agreed with Walling that, in her words, "the

Below: The NAACP opposed the activities of the Ku Klux Klan, including the widespread practice of lynching.

spirit of the abolitionists must be revived". Along with another civil rights activist, Henry Moskowitz, they met in New York in January 1909 and agreed to form the NAACP. Another member was W. E. B. Du Bois, the first African

Above: The NAACP's campaign for equality of treatment under the law finally succeeded in the 1950s.

American to obtain a doctorate from Harvard, who in 1910 became the NAACP's director of publicity and research. He was the founding editor of its principal publication, *The Crisis*. In the first issue, he defined its purpose: "To set forth those facts and arguments which show the danger of race prejudice, particularly as manifested today toward colored people." The NAACP became the major pressure group for black civil rights, leading protests against segregation wherever it existed, whether in Wilson's administration or in the South with its entrenched labyrinth of 'Jim Crow' laws. Its 45-year fight for racial justice led to the 1954 Supreme Court ruling that "separate but equal" facilities in the South were unconstitutional, a triumph for the "spirit of the abolitionists".

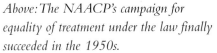

THE DEVELOPMENT OF SILENT FILM
ENTERTAINING AMERICA

California had a reliable climate in which to shoot movies and its scenery was exotic and varied, making it especially suitable for the increasingly popular genre of the Western. It was also a more favourable business environment: workers were less expensive to hire in what was already a labour-intensive industry. The land was cheaper for building studios, and it was far away from those dominating the fledgling industry in New York. After 1908, when the Motion Picture Patents Company attempted to monopolize the industry on the East Coast, independent film-makers escaped across the continent, settling in California, in a suburb of Los Angeles: Hollywood.

In 1910, D. W. Griffith, who had started his movie career as an actor and then a director with the Edison Moving Picture Company before moving to the Biograph Company, directed the first Hollywood movie, *In Old California*. It was not until the following year that the first film studio was established there. Other independents soon followed.

In 1913, Griffith returned to establish his own studio. Shortly after, he started work on the film that was to revolutionize the industry.

Released in 1915, Griffith's *Birth of a Nation* remains a landmark in the history of US cinema. It was the first Hollywood blockbuster, an epic tale of

Left: Griffith's The Birth of a Nation *proved the persuasive power of cinema.*

the Civil War and its aftermath, based on *The Clansman*, a novel by Thomas Dixon. Its claims to historical authenticity soon aroused great controversy. President Woodrow Wilson, after seeing it at the White House, allegedly remarked that it was like "writing history with lightning and my only regret is that it is all so terribly true". But its positive portrayal of the activities of the Ku Klux Klan led the NAACP to describe the film as "three miles of filth". For the audiences sitting in the darkness of nickelodeons across the United States, Griffith presented a version of the nation's past that was filtered through his own experiences growing up in rural poverty in the post-Civil War American South.

Hollywood became synonymous with film-making, and before long worldwide audiences could escape into the 'American Dream' simply by paying for a ticket to the movies.

NICKELODEON

The name 'nickelodeon' was coined by combining the price of admission – five cents – and the Greek word for a covered theatre. All over the United States, and particularly in the cities, these small neighbourhood cinemas screened the latest Hollywood productions. The films were silent, so newly arrived immigrants with limited command of the language could still enjoy the melodramas and slapstick comedies, without having to concentrate on dialogue. Nickelodeons brought movies as popular entertainment to the American masses.

Right: Piano accompaniment added to the impact of silent movies.

WOODROW WILSON

1913–1921

Woodrow Wilson believed in the ideal of democracy. He led the nation into World War I because he was convinced that "the world must be made safe for democracy". Determined that "peace must be planted upon the tested foundations of political liberty", he was the architect of an international organization that aimed to avert future conflicts. Like Theodore Roosevelt, President Wilson was awarded the Nobel Peace Prize. The United States initially rejected his vision, retreating into isolationism. Nevertheless his idealism would still influence US foreign policy and the rhetoric of his successors as the United States aspired to fulfil the destiny Wilson had envisaged for it: spreading its democratic values throughout the world.

EARLY LIFE

He was born in 1856 in Staunton, Virginia. Eight months before his fifth birthday, the state seceded from the Union: Thomas Woodrow Wilson's early childhood memories were of war.

Born: 28 December 1856, Staunton, Virginia

Parents: Joseph (1822–1903) and Jessie (1826–88)

Family background: Presbyterian ministry

Education: College of New Jersey (Princeton) (1879)

Johns Hopkins PhD (1886)

Religion: Presbyterian

Occupation: Academic, public service

Military service: None

Political career: Governor of New Jersey, 1911–13

Presidential annual salary: $75,000

Political party: Democrat

Died: 3 February 1924, Washington DC

His father was a Presbyterian minister, originally from Ohio, who, upon moving to the South in 1849, became a convert to the Confederate cause. His mother, from whom he gained his middle name, and the one by which he preferred to be known, was a minister's daughter. Wilson's character was shaped by his family's strong Christian values.

At 16 he went to Davidson College in North Carolina, but ill health – he had never been physically robust – contributed to his decision to drop out after a year. In 1875, he went north, enrolling at the College of New Jersey, yet to be renamed Princeton University. Four years later, he graduated and began to study law, eventually qualifying as a lawyer in Georgia and setting up a practice in Atlanta. It was the wrong career choice. Within a year he had returned to study for a doctoral degree in political science and history at Johns Hopkins University. Wilson's academic career progressed through appointments at Bryn Mawr College and Wesleyan University. His publications on US government and politics were well received. In 1890 he returned to his

Left: As the United States became a world power, Woodrow Wilson imbued its foreign policy with an idealistic fervour and a missionary ambition to spread the values of US democracy abroad.

alma mater in New Jersey. Six years later it became Princeton University, and in 1902 Professor Wilson was chosen as its 13th president.

Initially popular with both the University's trustees and its faculty, his plans to reform Princeton bitterly divided both the academic community and the graduates, whose continuing financial commitment to the institution was often based on their nostalgic affection for its traditions.

POLITICAL CAREER

In the 1910 mid-term elections he left academic life, graduating to state politics as New Jersey's first Democrat governor for 14 years. Two years later, Wilson, the Southerner who had made his political career in the North, won his party's presidential nomination. Running on a reform platform, he beat both Taft and Theodore Roosevelt to become the first Democrat to win the White House in the 20th century.

The Democrats were no longer the party of the South: for the first time since the Civil War they controlled both Houses of Congress. Wilson was in no doubt as to who was responsible for his

---

ELLEN WILSON

Born in Georgia in 1860 and married to Woodrow Wilson in 1885, Ellen Axson, like her husband, came from a Presbyterian minister's family. They had three children. Her strong social conscience led her to work to improve the slum conditions in which many of Washington's black community lived. She died from kidney failure in 1914.

Above: The passengers of the luxury liner Lusitania *were unaware that it carried a deadly cargo of munitions.*

victory. He told William McCombs, his campaign manager, "Remember that God ordained that I should be President of the United States."

RADICAL REFORM

Not since John Adams had addressed Congress in person in 1797 had a president come to Capitol Hill as Wilson did in April 1913, a month after his inauguration, to enlist support for his progressive legislative agenda. He confronted head-on the issues that had divided generations of US politicians: tariff reform, the currency and the banking system. Within the year, Wilson achieved the first significant reduction in the tariff in almost 70 years, moving the United States towards accepting the benefits of free trade. He also signed legislation allowing him to appoint members to the Federal Reserve Board, which would exercise central control over the nation's banking system. In 1914, the Federal Trade Commission was established, with powers to intervene when businesses were suspected of abusing anti-trust laws.

Wilson's domestic legislative achievements during his first year in office consolidated his reputation both as a progressive and as a president prepared

to use the powers of his office to promote his reform agenda. When war broke out in Europe in August 1914, it would be the problem of how America should react to the conflict

that increasingly preoccupied its president. He also faced a personal tragedy: his wife, Ellen, died from kidney disease on 6 August.

OUTBREAK OF WAR

As the fighting in Europe escalated, Wilson argued for US neutrality. After the Cunard liner *Lusitania* was sunk by a German torpedo in May 1915, with more than 1,000 passengers, including 128 Americans, losing their lives, the president demanded that Germany's indiscriminate submarine warfare should cease, involving the United States publically in the war. This proved too provocative for his secretary of state, William Jennings Bryan, who resigned over the issue. Wilson then made strenuous efforts to mediate between the European belligerents. He failed.

EDITH WILSON

Edith Bolling was born in Virginia in 1872. Her first husband, Norman Galt, died in 1908 and she married Wilson in 1915. Four years later, following his stroke, she began what she called her "stewardship" of his administration, determining the flow of public papers to him and acting as his intermediary with the Cabinet. She successfully kept the American people unaware of his incapacity for the remainder of their time in the White House. Her last public appearance was at John F. Kennedy's inauguration in 1961. She died later that year, on the 105th anniversary of her late husband's birth.

Below: Edith Bolling Galt may well have been the 'first woman to run the American government', during the debilitating illness of her husband.

In December 1915, he married Edith Bolling Galt. The following year he became the first Democrat to be elected to two consecutive terms in the White House since Andrew Jackson.

SECOND ADMINISTRATION

In February 1917, Germany abandoned any commitment to restrict the operations of its submarines. Neutral vessels – including US ships – were counted as legitimate targets. At the same time, the German foreign minister, Arthur Zimmermann, instructed his ambassador in Mexico to suggest that if the US abandoned its neutrality, Germany would help Mexico "reconquer" territory lost during the Mexican-American war. The British intercepted his telegram and revealed its decoded content to the Americans. The following month, Wilson took the oath of office for a second time. On 2 April, he asked Congress to declare war against Germany. The United States would help to "bring peace and safety to all nations and make the world itself at last free". Although US troops did not begin crossing the Atlantic in numbers until the following year, the potential military resources that the United States offered its European allies helped to hasten the end of the war.

In January 1918, Wilson outlined the basis of a peace settlement in which European empires should respect the rights of those whom they ruled. The organizing principle of his 'Fourteen Points' was the idea of "justice to all peoples and nationalities, and their right to live on equal terms of liberty and safety with one another, whether they be strong or weak". The following year Wilson arrived in Paris to participate in the peace negotiations at Versailles. While he was there, he ignored representations from a French colonial subject, Ho Chi Minh, who had been

Right: Army officers stand on chairs to see into the room where the Treaty of Versailles is being signed on 28 June 1919.

FOURTEEN POINTS

Wilson's list of fourteen principles for a lasting peace included ending "private international understandings", ensuring freedom of navigation in international waters, promoting free trade, and encouraging disarmament. The president argued for the rights of colonial peoples to be recognized and proposed solutions to the specific disputes over territory that had led Europe into war. He also advanced his idea of "a general association of nations" to guarantee "political independence and territorial integrity" for all the nations of the world.

inspired by his democratic rhetoric to request help in liberating his country from imperial control. Many years later, Vietnam would demand rather more of the USA's attention.

European leaders had different agendas as they discussed the terms and conditions of the Treaty of Versailles. They had no intention of deferring to the democratic idealism of the president of the United States when it came to the details of the settlement, although they did accept his proposal to establish the League of Nations.

When Wilson left Europe it was with a treaty that many Americans thought betrayed the principles for which they had been persuaded to fight, and the country was now in no mood to give its support to his international organization for preserving peace. The postwar reaction at home was isolationism: the United States was reluctant to involve itself with international politics. It was this that undermined the architecture of the League of Nations, Wilson's vision for a lasting democratic peace.

Taking his case to the people caused Wilson's health to collapse. He suffered a massive stroke, and was no longer capable of taking part in the administration of the country. It became Washington's best-kept secret: for more than a year his wife and closest advisers maintained the charade that he was still in control. The world was one that he no longer understood. The United States rejected the Treaty of Versailles, the League of Nations and international engagement; instead it prepared to indulge itself in the heady materialism of the 1920s.

Despite this defeat, Wilson had achieved great things. His liberal progressivism brought about significant economic and social reforms. He was opposed to prohibition, which became law during his last year in office. He once wrote: "The President is at liberty both in law and conscience to be as big as he can." Woodrow Wilson had tried his best to live up to his ideal.

WORLD WAR I
1914–1918

When Congress declared war on Germany on 6 April 1917, the United States was not ready for a fight. Given the casualties being inflicted on the killing fields of Europe at the time, the regular army could muster only enough troops to take part in a single battle. The United States mobilized. Like Abraham Lincoln before him, Woodrow Wilson assumed a broad range of executive powers to lead the nation into war.

In May 1917, Congress passed the National Conscription Act. Few had volunteered immediately for active service. Now, on 5 June 1917, all men aged between 21 and 30 were required to register for the draft. A wave of patriotic fervour persuaded 10 million to do so; by the end of the war, another 14 million Americans had joined them.

Their commander was John 'Black Jack' Pershing. His nickname derived from his command of a regiment of black troops in Cuba. Among the forces he led in France would be more than 350,000 African-Americans who,

Below: Uncle Sam, the personification of the United States, calls the people to arms to join the war effort.

although they fought in segregated units, found that Europe was more racially tolerant than the USA, as well as being receptive to their music: jazz. They returned to the United States with renewed demands for the recognition of their civil rights.

Pershing and the first units of the American Expeditionary Force arrived in France in June 1917, with orders from the secretary of war that included the requirement "to co-operate with the forces of the other countries … But in so doing the underlying idea must be kept in view that the forces of the United States are a separate and distinct component of the combined forces, the

Above: General Pershing arrives in France with the first US troops to fight in World War I.

identity of which must be preserved." This, together with delays caused by the need to train Americans in the tactics of trench warfare, caused friction between the allies.

For the British and French, US replacements in existing units would mean a fresh infusion of troops in a grim war of attrition. Pershing resisted this idea: he wanted his forces to operate effectively and independently in battle. In October 1917 he did allow some battalions to spend short periods of time

alongside a French division. Three soldiers were killed: the first US casualties of the war.

It was not until the spring of 1918 that US infantrymen, known as 'dough-boys' (there is no definitive explanation for this nickname), participated in battlefield action. On 20 April in the Lorraine region of France, the 26th Division fought to defend and then regain the village of Seicheprey. In May, US troops fought at Cantigny and in June at Chateau-Thierry and Belleau Wood. They were also involved in the second Battle of the Marne during the last major German offensive. By 4 July Pershing commanded a million troops in France, a number set to double during the following four months. General Pershing's army could now fight as equals beside those of France and Britain against the depleted and war-weary Germans.

In October, it was the US president whom the German Chancellor first approached with the proposal of an armistice. In answer to Wilson's request for clarification, Germany accepted the terms outlined in his 'Fourteen Points' speech of the previous January. Wilson's reply recognized that it would be the Allies who would dictate how the war would end, and if the United States was to respond to "the military masters and ... autocrats of Germany now, or if it is likely to have to deal with them later in regard to the international obligations of the German Empire, it must demand, not peace negotiations but surrender".

The following month it was all over. With Germany in the throes of revolution, the armistice was signed on 11 November. US casualties stood at more than 300,000 in a war that had cost the lives of 8.5 million – the 'Lost Generation'. General Pershing and the American Expeditionary Force returned to the United States as heroes. On his retirement, he was given the title 'General of the Armies'. He died in July 1948, having witnessed another war in which US troops gave their lives fighting for the same ideal as those who had joined him on the battlefields of France in 1918.

Above: In August 1918, US forces planned their first independent action, at St Mihiel, France. Their limited offensive was successful, although the retreating Germans burnt down the town. Three months later the war ended when the armistice was signed.

US PARTICIPATION IN WORLD WAR I

1917

6 April: The United States declares war on Germany

25 June: First US Troops land in France

1918

8 January: Woodrow Wilson sets out his plan for peace in Europe ('Fourteen Points')

11 November: Armistice ends fighting in Europe

1919

18 January: Peace conference opens at Versailles

25 January: Proposal for League of Nations accepted

THE TREATY OF VERSAILLES
AND THE LEAGUE OF NATIONS

Having crossed the Atlantic on the USS *George Washington* the month after the armistice had been signed, Woodrow Wilson was the first president to meet with his counterparts in France, Britain and Italy face to face. The US idealist encountered European realists.

Wilson joined the European leaders in Paris to take part in the great power bargaining that would shape the Treaty of Versailles and enshrine his vision of the League of Nations. His political base at home had been shaken after the Republicans regained control of Congress in the 1918 mid-term elections. Worse was to come. Despite his widespread international popularity – the result of his clear commitment to the principles of a democratic peace – and the air of hopeful expectation that accompanied his arrival in Europe, Wilson and his allies sat down to

Below: Vittorio Orlando (second left) walked out of the Versailles negotiations. The remaining Allied leaders agreed the terms of peace.

negotiate in an atmosphere of mutual misunderstanding, their attitudes moulded by their different experiences of the war.

The French president, Georges Clemenceau, aged 77, had twice witnessed the consequences of German belligerence: the invasion of his country during the Franco-Prussian war of 1871 and the carnage of the previous four years of fighting on French soil. He was determined that the defeated enemy should no longer threaten its European neighbours. Britain's liberal prime minister, Lloyd George, came to Versailles having won an election on the promises to 'Hang the Kaiser' and 'Make Germany Pay'. More than five million Britons had served in France and almost half that number had become casualties of war. Lloyd George was prepared to compromise, but not at any price.

Italy had changed sides during the war. Vittorio Orlando, who had, ironically, become prime minister as a result of his country's heavy defeat at the hands of the Germans in the Battle of

Above: British prime minister Lloyd George, French premier Georges Clemenceau and President Woodrow Wilson during talks at Versailles.

Caporetto in 1917, wanted control of the Croatian port of Fiume as a reward for joining the winners. He failed in his objective and took no further part in the discussions.

President Wilson held to his unwavering commitment to preserve his ideal of the League of Nations. He encountered scepticism in Paris and at the same time was being buffeted by political turbulence from his opponents back in the United States. Although he achieved his aim, it was at the expense of accepting his European allies' demands for a punitive peace.

Although the British prime minister and the French president almost came to blows at one stage, and were prevented only through the intervention of the American president, it was Lloyd George who presented himself as the pragmatist, bridging the Atlantic divide between Wilson, who was fired with missionary zeal, and Clemenceau, the stubborn defender of his national interests. Always adept at conjuring a

Right: An artist's impression of the United States of Europe, which might encourage world harmony and peace.

memorable image, when he was asked to rate his performance during the negotiations, Lloyd George described with characteristic self-confidence how he felt he had done: "Not badly, considering I was seated between Jesus Christ and Napoleon."

The Versailles negotiations satisfied no one, least of all the Germans, who were excluded from them. They were presented with crippling demands for reparations and the loss of territory they had held before the war. Wilson was forced to accept his co-signatories' territorial demands and the punitive terms of the peace. On his less than triumphant return to the United States, he personally presented the treaty to the Senate. It would be sent back to him, unratified. The League of Nations, the Covenant for which he had fought so tenaciously to include in the Treaty of Versailles, would go ahead but without US involvement.

THE LEAGUE OF NATIONS

It was not only the Americans who did not join. Germany, defeated and humiliated, was excluded. So too was Russia: its new communist leaders were not

invited to be members of the international organization, which from January 1920 was based in Geneva. The League's mission was "to promote international co-operation and to achieve international peace and security", but with three major powers relegated to the sidelines, its chances of promoting global harmony were slim. It was a forum for the diplomatic resolution of international conflict, backed by the threat of economic sanctions, but it had no independent military force that could act in

a peacekeeping capacity. Successful in encouraging co-operation between nations in the areas of health and welfare policies, the League failed to prevent what many saw as the inevitable outcome of the treaty agreed in Paris in 1919. Two decades after Wilson's transatlantic voyage to Versailles, Europe went to war once more.

Below: Those who agreed the Treaty of Versailles and ended World War I soon saw their efforts undermined by events.

THE PALESTINIAN MANDATE

In 1922, the League of Nations gave the British government a mandate to govern Palestine. It recognized the need for "a national home for the Jewish people", a commitment independently endorsed by Congress. To honour wartime pledges to the Arabs, Britain divided the mandate, creating the Transjordan, an area where Jewish settlement was forbidden. These conflicting priorities fuelled the competing and irreconcilable claims of Arabs and Jews for sovereignty over the territory.

PROHIBITION
1920

The Eighteenth Amendment to the Constitution famously failed in its attempt to prevent Americans drinking alcohol. Prohibition was introduced for medical, social, political and economic reasons. It was agreed by Congress in December 1917, and its introduction banned "the manufacture, sale, or transportation of intoxicating liquors" in the United States as well as prohibiting their import and export to and from the country. After ratification by the states, many of which had already introduced measures banning the production and sale of alcohol, legislation was necessary to enforce the amendment. A teetotal member of the House of Representatives, Andrew Volstead, gave his name to the act, which was passed by Congress on 28 October 1919, ushering in the age of national prohibition.

President Woodrow Wilson, who was still incapacitated in the immediate aftermath of his stroke, opposed the Volstead Act, but Congress immediately overturned his veto. Prohibition went into effect in January 1920. While he was in favour of temperance, Wilson, like many others at the time, saw that a constitutional amendment would not

ANTI-SALOON LEAGUE

The Anti-Saloon League was the main pressure group advocating the prohibition of alcohol. It began life as a state society, founded in 1893 at Oberlin College, Ohio. The idea was taken up in other states and it became a national society in 1895. It was organized along business lines, and took a sophisticated approach to public relations, publishing its own newspapers to persuade the public of the evils of alcohol.

Backed by ministers and congregations of various Protestant denominations, particularly the Methodists, the League aimed to achieve temperance through legislation, and gained considerable political influence through its backing of 'dry' candidates – those who were prepared to vote for prohibition, regardless of whether they themselves were teetotal – in local and state elections. It began its successful campaign for national prohibition in 1913.

Above: Leaders of the Anti-Saloon League fought for an alcohol-free society. They argued for temperance and campaigned for the constitutional amendment which banned the production, sale and transportation of alcohol throughout the United States.

Below: Illegal distilleries proliferated on the streets to serve the trade of the speakeasies.

Below: Government officials smash illegal barrels of alcohol, although it was common practice to bribe the police to turn a blind eye.

Above: Methods of transporting illegal alcohol from rural distilleries to the towns were ingenious: the activity became almost unstoppable.

stop Americans consuming alcohol. When he left the White House in 1921, Wilson took his private stock of Scotch whiskey and fine wine with him.

Some of those prepared to become bootleggers, to open speakeasies, to make moonshine or to risk smuggling alcohol between states became rich and famous. In Chicago, there were few who believed that Al Capone made his living, as he claimed on his business card, from dealing in furniture.

Above: Speakeasies were illegal drinking dens that operated and flourished during the era of prohibition.

Joseph P. Kennedy, the son of a former Boston saloon-keeper, amassed a large fortune during the 1920s and among his business connections were those who were profiting from the opportunities that prohibition created.

Henry Ford was prominent among those business leaders who supported prohibition: he claimed that he would rather close down his production line than see the legislation repealed. Others, such as Henry Joy, president of the Packard Motor Car Company, who had been active in the Anti-Saloon League, eventually admitted that they had made a mistake. In 1925 Joy wrote: "I was stupidly wrong. America must open its eyes and recognize that human nature cannot be changed by legal enactment."

Eight years later, Congress and the president came to agree with him. Although legislation forbidding alcohol would remain in force in a number of states, in 1933 Franklin Roosevelt signed the Twenty-first Amendment, bringing national prohibition to an end.

Right: The Eighteenth Amendment did not make it illegal to drink spirits; it was the manufacture, sale and distribution that the law disallowed.

BOOTLEGGERS, SPEAKEASIES AND MOONSHINE

Prohibition produced its own industrial language. Bootleggers (named after smugglers who carried contraband in the legs of their boots) acted as suppliers, carrying alcohol from rural distilleries to urban centres, or importing it from abroad. Liquor was retailed in speakeasies: illicit bars where it was still possible to enjoy a drink. The substitute for whiskey as the drink of choice was moonshine, which home-made stills produced in quantities to supply a thirsty nation. Problems of quality control were ignored by its makers, distributors, retailers and consumers alike.

Below: Producing alcohol for a thirsty nation was big business, and encouraged criminal activity.

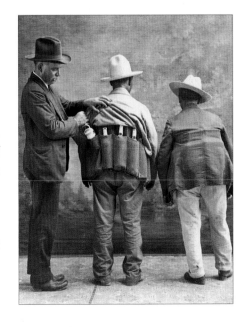

CHAPTER TWO

WARREN HARDING TO FRANKLIN D. ROOSEVELT

1921–1945

BETWEEN THE TWO WORLD WARS, THREE DIFFERENT REPUBLICANS WON A PRESIDENTIAL ELECTION EACH. FROM 1932–44 ONE DEMOCRAT WON FOUR: FRANKLIN DELANO ROOSEVELT, THE MASTER POLITICIAN OF 'THE AMERICAN CENTURY'. THE OPTIMISM AND ENERGY OF THE 'ROARING TWENTIES' CAME TO A SHATTERING END AS THE STOCK MARKET IMPLODED, LOSING $30 BILLION IN VALUE IN THE WALL STREET CRASH, AND BOOM BECAME BUST. THE UNITED STATES STRUGGLED THROUGH THE DEPRESSION OF THE 1930S, DESPITE THE OPTIMISM SURROUNDING THE NATIONAL RECOVERY PROGRAMME OF ROOSEVELT'S 'NEW DEAL'. BY THE END OF WORLD WAR II, THE USA'S POSITION OF INTERNATIONAL PRE-EMINENCE WAS CONFIRMED. THE INVENTION OF NUCLEAR WEAPONS DIRECTED THE WAY TO A HIGH-RISK FUTURE. PRESIDENTS KNEW THAT ORDERING THEIR USE COULD MEAN THE END OF THE WORLD. AT THE SAME TIME, THE IDEALISM OF WOODROW WILSON WAS SEEN AGAIN IN THE CREATION OF THE UNITED NATIONS.

Left: The Wall Street Crash of 1928 is remembered as one of the most infamous days in the history of share trading.

WARREN HARDING
1921–1923

President Warren Harding felt that "normalcy" was what the country needed after the energy of progressivism and the trauma of war. In his inaugural address he suggested that Americans "must strive for normalcy to achieve stability". Harding then settled into a leadership style that allowed him time to indulge his habitual leisure pursuits: golf, poker and extra-marital affairs.

Born in 1865, a few months after the end of the Civil War, Harding graduated from Ohio Central College at the age of 17. He had been editor of the campus newspaper, and in 1884, with the help of a couple of friends, he bought the *Marion Star* newspaper, which became the platform for his subsequent political career. In 1891, Harding married Florence Kling De Wolfe, a wealthy divorcée. They had children, but not with each other: hers was a son by her former husband; his would be a daughter by Nan Britton, one of his long-term mistresses. In 1899

Above: Warren Harding was the first 20th-century chief executive to die from natural causes while in office.

Harding entered the Ohio State Senate as a Republican, beginning a career in public life that spluttered along until his election to the federal Senate in 1914 and to the White House six years later.

Some of his Cabinet choices – Charles Hughes as secretary of state, Andrew Mellon as treasury secretary and Herbert Hoover as secretary of commerce – were very good. On the other hand, his crony Harry Daugherty, who became attorney general, was comprehensively dishonest, and Albert Fall, the secretary for the interior, took bribes in return for allowing oil companies to exploit the government's oil reserve in Teapot Dome, Wyoming. "Normalcy" seemed to mean a return to the widespread corruption of the Grant administration.

In 1923, and in failing health, Harding set out on a 'Voyage of Understanding' across the USA, intended to deflect the mounting criticism of his presidency as it creaked under the weight of scandal. On 2 August, aged 57, he died from natural causes in a San Francisco hotel, although unsubstantiated rumours claimed he had been poisoned. Warren Harding was simply unsuited to the office he held with such lack of distinction. It was, as he once said, "a hell of a job".

FLORENCE HARDING

Born in Ohio in 1860, Florence Kling eloped at 19 with her first husband, Henry De Wolfe, who was an alcoholic. They had one son and divorced in 1886. By then she had met Warren Harding, whom she married five years later. She helped make his newspaper profitable and supported his political career, campaigning indefatigably when he ran for president. As first lady, her common touch made her popular. She died in 1924, a year after her husband's death in office.

Below: The Harding administration began cutting income tax to boost the post-war economy.

Born: 2 November 1865, Corsica, Ohio
Parents: George (1844–1928) and Phoebe (1843–1910)
Family background: Medicine
Education: Ohio Central College (1882)
Religion: Baptist
Occupation: Newspaper editor and publisher
Military service: None
Political career: Ohio State Senate, 1900–4
Lieutenant governor of Ohio, 1904–6
US Senate, 1915–21
Presidential annual salary: $75,000
Political party: Republican
Died: 2 August 1923, San Francisco, California

VOTES FOR WOMEN

They protested, they picketed and they petitioned. During the 19th century, many who supported the cause of abolitionism and the demand for civil rights connected the case for racial equality with the call for women's rights. In 1848, at Seneca Falls, Elizabeth Cady Stanton argued for women's suffrage. After the Civil War, she found a formidable ally in Susan B. Anthony, who in 1872 managed to vote in the presidential election before being arrested and fined. She refused to pay and remained an indefatigable campaigner until her death at the age of 86 in 1906.

By the end of the 19th century women had gained the right to vote in several of the new western states, including Colorado, Idaho, Wyoming and Utah. As the progressive era took shape, the campaign gained momentum. Alice Paul and Lucy Burns adopted the more militant tactics they had witnessed while visiting the United Kingdom. Mass demonstrations and organized picketing, including a daily protest outside the White House, made sure that the issue remained high on the political agenda. Paul and Burns were arrested. After going on hunger strikes, they were force-fed.

In 1915, Carrie Chapman Catt began a second term as president of the National American Woman Suffrage Association. She campaigned to force reform at state and federal level. In 1917, New York became the first East Coast state to give women the vote. Two years later Congress finally passed the Nineteenth Amendment to the

Above: Alice Paul unfurls a banner from the balcony of the National Women's Party headquarters, showing a star for each state that has ratified the Nineteenth Amendment giving women the right to vote.

Constitution, introduced in 1878, which declared: "The right of citizens of the United States to vote shall not be denied or abridged by the United States or by any State on account of sex."

Ratification was achieved in time for women to cast their ballots in the 1920 presidential election. One who did so was Charlotte Woodward, aged 81, who was by then the sole survivor of the Seneca Falls Convention. As Carrie Chapman Catt put it in 1924, the women's suffrage movement had been "an effort to bring men to feel less superior and women to feel less inferior". Much had been achieved: more was left to do.

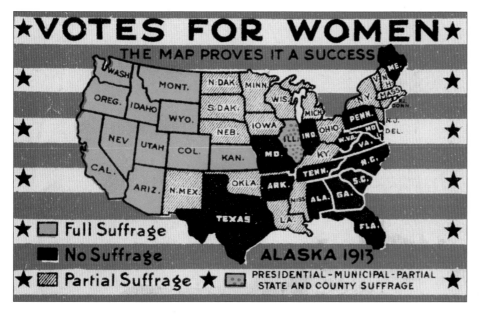

Left: A map of the USA indicating each state's position on women's suffrage in 1913.

THE DEVELOPMENT OF RADIO

In April 1922, the magazine *Telephony* informed its readers that: "President Harding has become one of the most enthusiastic radio telephone fans in Washington. Scarcely a day goes by that he does not 'listen-in' on the receiving set specially installed for him a short time ago by the wireless experts of the Navy Department." The previous month a pioneering radio station, KDKA in Pittsburgh, had broadcast the president's inaugural address, read simultaneously on air while he delivered the speech in Washington. Radio, as a medium of political communication and popular entertainment, seized the American imagination.

During World War I all US patents connected with the development of radio had been consolidated to help the war effort, and equipment was produced solely for the military. The Radio Corporation of America (RCA) was

Below: The first president to make use of radio, Roosevelt's 'fireside chats' were broadcast to millions.

established at the end of the war under the direction of David Sarnoff. In 1921, it allowed listeners to witness the world heavyweight boxing championship fight between Jack Dempsey and Georges Carpentier. Three years later, there were radios in more than 2.5 million US homes. By the end of the decade, the National Broadcasting Corporation (NBC) had been created as a subsidiary of RCA and William Paley had established the rival Columbia Broadcasting System (CBS).

The networks of radio stations affiliated to NBC and CBS provided a way for politicians to speak directly to the whole nation, rather than having their words transcribed, with editorial comments added, and read in newspapers. Franklin Roosevelt broadcast a long series of 'fireside chats', which served to shrink the distance between the president and the people. His first broadcast was made in March 1933, just over a week after he had taken office, and he continued the practice throughout his presidency: the last 'fireside chat'

Above: Radio, developed for the armed services in times of war, quickly became a source of popular entertainment.

took place in June 1944. During these talks he became a temporary guest in US homes.

Roosevelt used radio to reassure the nation in the depths of the Depression. Later he used it again to explain the need for America to go to war once more. He demonstrated that a president could achieve better ratings than many contemporary entertainment shows.

Radio audiences trusted what they heard. On 31 October 1938, the actor Orson Welles spooked the USA, broadcasting a live adaptation of H. G. Wells's story *The War of the Worlds* on CBS. Presenting the first part of the drama as a series of news bulletins, Welles convinced his audience that the United States was in the throes of an invasion from Mars. The reaction of the listeners dramatized the power of the medium, and showed how those adept at using it could influence their audience. As Roosevelt reportedly told Welles, there were two great actors in the USA at that time. Welles was the other one.

CALVIN COOLIDGE
1923–1929

When the writer Dorothy Parker was told that President Calvin Coolidge had died, she famously asked: "How could they tell?" Coolidge would have appreciated her witticism. He liked people to laugh. He allowed himself to be photographed in relaxed poses and in a variety of costumes that his advisors warned might make him look ridiculous. Coolidge knew better. His lack of affectation was a political asset; so too was his transparent integrity as he inherited the White House after the scandal-mired years of his predecessor Harding's administration.

Born in Vermont on Independence Day in 1872, Coolidge graduated from Amherst College in Massachusetts and became a lawyer, opening a practice in

Above: Coolidge's honesty restored public faith in the presidency, but his leadership remained uninspiring.

nearby Northampton in 1897. In 1905 he married Grace Goodhue, and they had two sons. Two years later, as a Republican, he was elected to the State Legislature. In 1910 he returned to Northampton as mayor. Having served in the state Senate, and as both lieutenant governor and governor of Massachusetts, he entered national politics as Harding's vice president. It was just before midnight on 2 August that he received the news of the president's sudden death. His father, a justice of the peace, with whom he was staying at the time, administered the oath of office and Coolidge went back to bed.

He remained untainted by the scandals that had emerged during Harding's administration and which eventually ended the career of Harry Daugherty as attorney general, though his image of absolute integrity could not disguise his limitations as a leader. With the economy buoyant and his party rallying behind him, Coolidge

won the Republican nomination in 1924 and was elected president in his own right.

Thereafter he did little to impress, introducing no domestic legislation of significance and issuing no public statements to indicate his views on the major political questions of the day. Coolidge presided over the rapid economic growth that characterized the 'Roaring Twenties'. He and his treasury secretary, Andrew Mellon, believed in reducing the tax burden and minimizing federal expenditure, leaving such issues as employment legislation and economic controls to state governments. He was even reluctant to spend federal funds on flood control after the Mississippi flood of 1927.

His major achievement was to restore public confidence in the presidency. By avoiding giving offence to anyone Coolidge tried to remain popular with everyone. It came as a surprise when he announced in 1927 that he would not run for re-election. Unlike Theodore Roosevelt, he meant it. Honest but uninspiring, 'Silent Cal' left the White House and retired to his adopted state of Massachusetts where he died in 1933 at the age of 60.

Born: 4 July 1872, Plymouth, Vermont
Parents: John (1845–1926) and Victoria (1846–85)
Family background: Farming, store-keeping
Education: Amherst College (1895)
Religion: Congregationalist
Occupation: Lawyer
Military service: None
Political career: Northampton Ma. City Council, 1899
City solicitor, 1900–1
Clerk of courts, 1904
Massachusetts Legislature, 1907–8 and 1912–15
Mayor of Northampton, 1910–11,
Lieutenant governor of Massachusetts, 1916–18
Governor of Massachusetts, 1919–20
Vice president, 1921–3
Presidential annual salary: $75,000
Political party: Republican
Died: 5 January 1933, Northampton, Massachusetts

GRACE COOLIDGE

From Vermont, Grace Goodhue was born in 1879 and married Calvin Coolidge in 1905. She had two sons, the eldest of whom died at the age of 16 while the family was living in the White House. Her charm and vivacity compensated for her husband's dour demeanour. She helped raise $2 million for the Clarke School for the Deaf in her adopted home town of Northampton in Massachusetts. After her husband died, she lived on for 24 years, dying in 1957 at the age of 78.

THE SCOPES TRIAL
1925

If a more modern, secular US society seemed to be in the making, it was not without its opponents. In July 1925, God went on trial in a courtroom in a small town in Tennessee. The three-time losing Democrat candidate for the presidency, William Jennings Bryan, argued with one of the most famous trial lawyers of the day, Clarence Darrow. Should the theory of evolution be taught as fact, challenging the biblical account of creation? John Scopes, a Dayton high school science teacher, was prosecuted for telling his students, in the words of one of them, "all about monkeys and things".

Scopes was found guilty and fined. That was no surprise: he had freely admitted his action in order to allow the proceedings to take place. In due course an appeal court overturned the verdict and dismissed "this bizarre case", which had seized the national imagination. The real issue was a profound and enduring clash of two cultures: scientific rationalism and religious conviction.

Charles Darwin's publication of *The Origin of Species* in 1859 and *The Descent of Man* in 1871 had introduced a scientific explanation for what had always been a matter of faith. The theory of evolution rippled outwards, and was applied to economic life as well as the natural world. 'Social Darwinism' with its accompanying mantra – 'the survival of the fittest' – justified the competitive capitalism of the Gilded Age, in which the strong prospered and the weakest were left behind. The process of natural selection was thought to ensure a healthier and wealthier society.

William Jennings Bryan had opposed such ideas throughout his political career. Championing the poor and the dispossessed, he had argued eloquently for economic and social reform. He agreed with those who accepted the Bible as literal truth and whose beliefs had coined a term: fundamentalism.

The Scopes trial allowed Americans to debate the place of religion in a modern secular society. The high point of the trial came when Darrow cross-examined Bryan, forcing him to admit that biblical stories were open to interpretation. Taking no comfort from the verdict, fundamentalists withdrew from the political arena for the next half century and appeared to be in retreat, only to re-emerge at the end of the 20th century as a formidable force in US presidential politics.

Below: The Scopes trial was a landmark case, but the teaching of evolution in US classrooms remains controversial.

MOUNT RUSHMORE

1927

On Mount Rushmore in South Dakota the heads of four presidents are carved from stone. It is, as President Calvin Coolidge said at the dedication ceremony on 10 August 1927, "decidedly American in conception, in its magnitude, in its meaning and altogether worthy of our Country". Theodore Roosevelt, the most contentious choice, appears between Thomas Jefferson and Abraham Lincoln. George Washington is more prominent.

The original idea had been more modest: a mountain sculpture of figures from the history of the West – Lewis and Clark, George Armstrong Custer, Buffalo Bill and the Native Americans they encountered there – designed to encourage tourism. But when the sculptor Gutzon Borglum was enlisted to work on the project, he had something far greater in mind. As the nation approached the 150th anniversary of the Philadelphia Convention, the memorial would symbolize the

Right: Gutzon Borglum working on the first model of the gigantic memorial.

contributions of four presidents to the establishment, growth, preservation and greatness of the United States.

For Coolidge, Washington "represents our independence, our Constitution, our liberty". Jefferson "embodied the spirit of expansion" and Lincoln had championed "the principle of freedom to all inhabitants of our land". Why should Theodore Roosevelt, Coolidge's fellow Republican, but a far more controversial and contemporary figure – he had died only eight years previously – share such company? According to Coolidge, Roosevelt had championed economic freedom as well as political liberty,

Above: An enduring icon, the carved stone masterpiece in the side of a mountain has immortalized four of the United States most respected presidents for ever. From left to right: Washington, Jefferson, Theodore Roosevelt and Lincoln.

and in the construction of the Panama Canal he had "realized the vision that inspired Columbus in his search for a new passage to the orient".

In the depths of the Depression, funding the work was a problem. By 1941 it was almost complete. Borglum died on 6 March and his son Lincoln, named for the Great Emancipator, spent the next seven months adding the finishing touches: carving was completed on 31 October.

Mount Rushmore endures as a monument not only to the presidents whose achievements it celebrates, but also to the ambition of those whose vision and persistence transformed the landscape of the Black Hills of South Dakota forever. Their enduring legacy was the creation of what remains, quite simply, the largest work of art on earth.

J. EDGAR HOOVER AND THE FBI

In 1924 J. Edgar Hoover (who was no relation to President Herbert Hoover) was appointed as the sixth director of the Federal Bureau of Investigation, which had been set up in 1908. He was to remain in the post for nearly 50 years. Knowing that information brought job security as well as power, he was rumoured to keep files of in-criminating information on the eight presidents at whose pleasure – more often displeasure – he served, ensuring that he remained politically untouch-able until he died, still in office, in 1972.

ORIGINS OF THE FBI

In 1803, the same year that his eldest brother, Napoleon, sold the Louisiana Territory to Thomas Jefferson, Jerome Bonaparte, on a visit to the United States, married an American, Elizabeth Patterson. Napoleon refused to agree to the match. Having accompanied her husband to Europe, Elizabeth returned without him to her home in Baltimore with their infant son, named for his father. Just over a century later, her grandson, Charles, would become attorney general in the administration of Theodore Roosevelt. He was the

Below: Fear of communism was rife in 1919. This cartoon depicts Bolshevism and anarchy creeping under the flag.

Above: Hoover became synonymous with the government department he led. No president dared to fire him.

driving force behind the creation of the organization that became the Federal Bureau of Investigation.

Charles Bonaparte identified a problem. The Justice Department had "no … permanent detective force under its immediate control". He therefore set one up, and at the end of his term in office he suggested the creation of a permanent team of inves-tigators attached to the department. Under his successor, George Wicker-sham, the team became known as the Bureau of Investigation. In its early days, there was little to investigate, because most crimes violated state rather than federal laws. Gradually, however, the Bureau's sphere of activity broadened: during World War I it was involved in cases of espionage, draft evasion, sabotage and the activities of those classed as 'enemy aliens'. Prohibition boosted not only the level of criminal activity, but also the opportunities for the Bureau to involve itself in more high-profile cases, particularly under its new director, J. Edgar Hoover.

THE PALMER RAIDS

John Edgar Hoover was born on New Year's Day, 1895, in Washington DC. After graduating from George Wash-ington University with a law degree, he began his government career in the Department of Justice in 1917. By the following year, he was an assistant to the attorney general, A. Mitchell Palmer.

Palmer's reaction to the wave of bombings that took place across the United States in 1919, in which, along with his family, he escaped injury as one of the explosions damaged his own house in Washington, produced a campaign against those who were allegedly planning a socialist revolution in the USA: the 'Red Scare'.

With Hoover as an enthusiastic accomplice directing operations, the attorney general launched a series of raids to round up suspected radicals and foreigners with scant regard for their civil rights. At first Palmer had the support of the public, but his credibility was undermined when the excesses of his actions were exposed. Nevertheless, in 1921 Hoover, who had benefited from the nationwide attention given to the raids, became assistant director of the Bureau of Investigation.

DIRECTOR OF THE FBI

Three years later, after a few months as acting director, Hoover was appointed to the position that he would hold for almost 48 years. At the time the Bureau employed about 450 special agents. In 1935, having been briefly renamed the Department of Investigation, it was formally given the title by which it has since been known: the Federal Bureau of Investigation. Hoover had already put his personal stamp on it, introducing new selection and training procedures. He carefully crafted the image of his special agents, or 'G-Men', as the resourceful crime-fighters of popular

Below: The Wall Street bombing in September 1920 killed 40 people and injured hundreds more.

G-MEN

George 'Machine Gun' Kelly, one of the most notorious prohibition gangsters, reputedly first used the term. In 1933, as FBI agents burst into a Memphis house to arrest him, he implored the 'G-Men' – government men – not to shoot. It became the stuff of legend and was popularized by Hollywood, notably in the James Cagney film *G Men* (1935), one of the gangster movies in which the Bureau's crime-fighting heroics were dramatized.

Right: G-Men came to prominence in the 1930s when the Bureau took on many high-profile federal cases.

myth, their exploits dramatized by Hollywood as they took on the gangsters and organized crime that thrived during the prohibition era.

Under Hoover's direction the FBI helped to shape the federal government's national security policies before, during and after World War II. The attitudes he had adopted as Palmer's assistant were the foundation for his own anti-communist crusade during the Cold War. For Hoover, fighting domestic subversion became an obsession. Anyone he saw as a radical was a threat. Those involved in the campaign for civil rights and the opponents of US military action overseas – notably during the Vietnam War – he deemed to be engaging in 'un-American activities'. Hoover identified them as legitimate targets of investigations that in many cases opened the FBI to charges of ignoring the civil liberties that were enshrined in the Bill of Rights.

Hoover was peerless as a bureaucratic survivor. His assumed knowledge of the potential embarrassments that littered the lives of prominent politicians and public officials, including successive presidents, none of whom dared to confront him, allowed him to remain the FBI's longest serving director.

When Hoover died in May 1972, his body lay in state in the Capitol building in Washington: an honour accorded to few Americans. His own private life, which had been the object of gossip and speculation while he lived, was soon investigated and exposed in lurid detail, overshadowing his long career as the nation's most famous G-Man.

HERBERT HOOVER
1929–1933

When the US stock market crashed in 1929, the president, along with many Americans, could not have realized either the depth or the length of the economic slump that would follow changing the landscape of US politics. Nevertheless, it was Herbert Hoover's inability to provide workable solutions to the problem as well as political leadership as the Depression took hold that led to him losing the presidency.

Hoover was the first 20th-century incumbent not to be re-elected, and the Republican party would not regain the White House for another 20 years. As president, he would be forever eclipsed by his successor, Franklin D. Roosevelt. Hoover, the former engineer and self-made millionaire, had encountered a problem he could not fix.

Born in Iowa in 1874 to Quaker parents, Hoover was an orphan by the age of nine. He travelled west to live with relatives in Oregon, and later went to Stanford University in San Francisco, where he was a member of the newly established college's first cohort of

Born: 10 August 1874, West Branch, Iowa

Parents: Jesse (1847–80) and Hulda (1848–83)

Family background: Orphaned aged nine; raised by uncle in Oregon

Education: Stanford University (1895)

Religion: Quaker

Occupation: Mining engineer

Military service: None

Political career: Secretary of commerce, 1921–8

Presidential annual salary: $75,000

Political party: Republican

Died: 20 October 1964, New York, New York

students. He graduated in 1895. His degree in geology opened the way to a career as a mining engineer, and he became an internationally renowned expert in his field. In 1899 he married Lou Henry, a fellow Stanford student. They had two children. The family travelled widely as Hoover's career took him to live and work in a number of countries, including Australia and China. By the age of 40 he had become rich through his consultancy work and ownership of profitable silver mines in Burma. He and his wife published their own translation of Georgius Agricola's

Above: A successful businessman turned politician, Hoover had his presidency wrecked by the USA's economic collapse.

classic 16th-century treatise on mining and metallurgy, *De Re Metallica*, which remains in print today.

Hoover was a progressive Republican and supported Theodore Roosevelt's bid to return to the White House in 1912. During World War I he took on a number of high-profile administrative tasks and relief work: he had been raised as a Quaker, and having achieved success in his career he wanted to focus on

Above: Dining on the edge of the abyss. Unable to prevent the USA toppling into the depression, Hoover, like many others, lost his job.

public service. He organized the evacuation from Europe of US civilians caught up in the conflict, oversaw the provision of humanitarian aid to Belgium and directed the US Food Administration, set up to supply the US army and its allies as well as domestic needs. His campaign for voluntary rationing in American households became known as 'Hooverizing'. After the war he co-ordinated US relief efforts aimed at rebuilding war-torn Europe, and he was with Woodrow Wilson as he negotiated the League of Nations and Peace Treaty at Versailles.

Hoover became secretary of commerce in Warren Harding's Cabinet, and is acknowledged to have been one of the president's few competent appointees. He remained in that position throughout Coolidge's administration, although their relationship was less than cordial. Hoover's popularity among Republicans and in the country at large enabled him to win the party's presidential nomination and the 1928 election. His opponent, Al Smith, was a Catholic and this caused the Democrats to lose the support of the 'solid South' for the first time since the end of reconstruction.

STOCK EXCHANGE CRISIS

Hoover had been in office a little over six months before 'Black Thursday'. On 24 October 1929, the New York Stock Exchange was jolted by a major fall in share prices. Five days later it was 'Black Tuesday' as the value of shares once more spiralled downwards, confirming the trend of the previous week. Wall Street had crashed, and the economic recession had arrived.

Hoover understood what had happened and coined the term 'Depression' to describe it. But he did not know how to deal with it, as the aftershocks of the USA's sudden plunge into economic reverse were felt around the world.

The banking system, never particularly robust, collapsed as banks failed across the nation. The downward spiral was aggravated by a severe drought in the summer of 1930, which hit the country's agricultural heartland and led to further defaulting on mortgages as well as food shortages.

Unemployment soared, reaching over 11 million in 1931. Hoover tried to stem the tide by pressing Congress

Below: Queues for work and for dole became a common sight as desperate people sought to keep home and family together.

to increase public expenditure to create jobs, with little success. With no federal system of welfare relief in place, poverty became widespread. In 1932, an army of unemployed veterans of World War I congregated in Washington to pressure Congress for advance payment of their war bonuses, which were not due for another 13 years. After scenes of rioting in the capital, General Douglas MacArthur defied the president's orders and used troops to clear the makeshift camps that the protesters had set up in Virginia, across the Potomac River from the White House – they were known as 'Hoovervilles'. Predictably, this move was a public relations disaster.

The United States' power to influence the course of international events was also diminished. In 1932, Japan invaded China and annexed Manchuria. Meanwhile, a state of political turmoil in Spain, Italy and Germany was paving the way for the emerging dictatorships in Europe.

Hoover ran for re-election more out of faith than conviction and was defeated comprehensively. An engineer who had more than demonstrated his humanitarian compassion when first he entered public life now left it because of his inability to show a common touch when confronted with an economic catastrophe that he, like many of his contemporaries, failed fully to understand. Herbert Hoover died in 1964 at the age of 90.

LOU HOOVER

Born in Iowa in 1874, she met her husband while both were geology students at Stanford. Lou Henry married Hoover in 1899 and they had two sons. They travelled extensively, and she became a proficient linguist. As first lady, she made regular radio broadcasts and speeches in support of her husband's policies. She died in 1944 at the age of 69.

CHARLES LINDBERGH
AND THE *SPIRIT OF ST LOUIS*

Charles Lindbergh was the first – and last – person to travel from New York to Paris in 33.5 hours sitting on a wicker chair. In May 1927, he flew across the Atlantic Ocean alone. His specially designed plane, the single-engine *Spirit of St Louis*, was made as light as possible to increase its flying range. His achievement made him a hero in Europe and in the United States, opening new horizons in the development of flight.

Born in Michigan in 1902, Lindbergh grew up in Minnesota. In 1920 he enrolled as an engineering student at the University of Wisconsin.

He dropped out, becoming a 'barn-stormer' or stunt pilot under the name 'Daredevil Lindbergh' and entertaining crowds by flying at fairs and airshows across America.

Following pilot training in the Army Air Service Reserve, he flew the mail between St Louis and Chicago. Attracted by the $25,000 prize offered for the first successful non-stop flight between New York and Paris, Lindbergh

Below: Just 20 years after flight was pioneered, Lindbergh made his ground-breaking record attempt to fly from New York to Paris in a single journey.

persuaded nine St Louis businessmen to invest in a plane that was capable of covering the distance. Named for its sponsors' home town, it was built in San Diego by the Ryan Aeronautical Company. When it was ready, Lindbergh flew it from California to New York, where he would take off on his transatlantic flight from Roosevelt Field. With an overnight stop in St Louis, he set a new record of 20 hours 21 minutes for the coast-to-coast journey.

THE RECORD FLIGHT

On 20 May at eight minutes before eight in the morning, Lindbergh left New York. Overcoming fog, ice, lack of sleep and hunger – he took only five sandwiches with him – he flew all day, through the night, and for most of the following day. Later he would recall at times almost skimming the ocean and, as he approached the Irish coast, shouting at a fisherman for directions, to no avail. Having found his way to Paris and circled the Eiffel Tower, he finally landed at the nearby Le Bourget airfield at 10.20 in the evening, local time, on 21 May. A large crowd had gathered to greet his arrival. The *New York Times* reported the historic event: "'Well, I made it,' smiled Lindbergh, as the little white monoplane came to a halt in the middle of the field." He became an instant international celebrity.

Lindbergh did not fly back. Returning on the USS *Memphis*, he travelled to Washington, where President Coolidge presented him with the Distinguished Flying Cross. A ticker-tape parade of unprecedented proportions greeted him in New York. Piloting the *Spirit of St Louis*, he embarked on a three-month nationwide tour. In March 1929, the president gave him the Congressional Medal of Honour. Two months later, Lindbergh married Anne Morrow, whom he had met when

day President Roosevelt ordered all government investigative agencies to co-operate with the New Jersey authorities in solving the crime. Two years later, Bruno Hauptmann, a German carpenter, was tried and executed for kidnap and murder, although controversy surrounded the conviction.

In 1935, the Lindberghs moved to Europe to escape incessant media attention. While there they made several trips to Germany, meeting members of its Nazi government, including Hermann Goering, from whom Lindbergh accepted a medal. In 1939, after his return to the United States, he became involved in the 'America First' movement, arguing against US involvement in World War II. Remarks suggestive of antisemitism and accusations of pro-Nazi sympathies damaged his credibility. Pearl Harbor undermined his argument. Lindbergh later served as a civilian advisor to American forces in the Pacific and flew around 50 combat missions. After the war he withdrew from public life. In 1974, he died at his home in Hawaii.

Below: The Nazi official Hermann Goering (centre) presented Lindbergh with a medal for his contribution to aviation.

Above: The success of the flight helped promote national pride, and Lindbergh received a hero's welcome on his return.

he had made a goodwill visit to Mexico, where her father was then the US ambassador.

KIDNAPPING AND AFTER

The fame Lindbergh had found as a solo pilot led to the defining moment of his family life. On 1 March 1932, the Lindberghs' eldest son, named for his father and then aged 20 months, was taken from their home in New Jersey. A number of ransom notes were received. J. Edgar Hoover offered his Bureau's assistance. On 12 May the baby's body was found. The following

THE WALL STREET CRASH
THE GREAT DEPRESSION, 1929

The stock market staggered, it tried to recover, then it collapsed. In the space of a week in October 1929, millions of US investors panicked. Economic confidence was shattered. The value of shares fell dramatically as sellers tried to stem their losses at any price. Those who had had the foresight to stop speculating before the crash – Joseph Kennedy was one of them – escaped with their fortunes intact. Many others lost everything.

On 31 December 1928, the Dow Jones Industrial Average, the index of the value of shares in leading industrial companies, had reached another all-time high, closing the day at 300 exactly. For many Americans, investing in the stock market seemed a one-way bet: a way of sharing in the economic wealth that the nation had generated throughout the decade of expansion and optimism that became known as the 'Roaring Twenties'. Hundreds of thousands of small investors took part, many borrowing more than half the value of the shares they were buying, accruing total loans of over $8.5 billion.

Three weeks after President Hoover's inauguration, on 25 March 1929, there was an ominous sign of what was

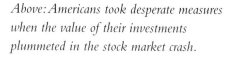

to come. The stock market tumbled in what the *New York Daily News* called a "selling avalanche". It rallied only after the banks intervened to provide cheaper credit for those who had borrowed to invest. By the summer it was business as usual again: the market reached record highs month after month.

Yet confidence proved to be brittle. In September, after the economist, Roger Babson, warned that, "Sooner or later, a crash is coming, and it may be terrific," Wall Street began to experience turbulence; in the following weeks the

Above: Americans took desperate measures when the value of their investments plummeted in the stock market crash.

market spiralled out of control. On 24 October – 'Black Thursday' – a wave of selling saw 13 million shares traded. Banks intervened, buying stocks in the hope of restoring equilibrium, and a late rally continued the following day. It was a short respite. Frenzied activity on 28 and 29 October – 'Black Monday' and 'Black Tuesday' – began a week in which the market lost $30 billion of its value, ten times the federal budget, and more than the United States had spent on its involvement in World War I. The Wall Street Crash became the defining event that marked the end of an era. It may not have caused the Depression, but it was a sign of the economic downturn that led to it.

Two months later the United States lurched into the 1930s, the decade of the Depression, the 'New Deal' and the leadership of one of its greatest presidents: Franklin Delano Roosevelt.

Left: The Wall Street Crash led to a nationwide run on the banks as widespread panic ensued.

FRANKLIN D. ROOSEVELT

1933–1945

When in his inaugural address in 1933 Roosevelt told Americans of his "firm belief that the only thing we have to fear is fear itself – nameless, unreasoning, unjustified terror which paralyzes needed efforts to convert retreat into advance," he was talking from experience. He spoke with the conviction that resulted from his long battle against the debilitating illness that had threatened his life. In 1921, at the age of 39, he contracted poliomyelitis. The disease was incurable, and – before the invention of the iron lung – if it caused paralysis of the chest it was fatal. He lost the use of his legs. His wife Eleanor said of him: "I know that he had real fear when he was first taken ill, but he learned to surmount it. After that I never heard him say he was afraid of anything." Franklin Roosevelt survived.

Born in 1882 at Hyde Park, the long-established family estate north of New York City, he was the only child of James Roosevelt and his second wife, Sara Delano. He spent his teenage years

Born: 30 January 1882, Hyde Park, New York

Parents: James (1828–1900) and Sara (1854–1941)

Family background: Business, landowning

Education: Harvard College (1903)

Religion: Episcopalian

Occupation: Public service

Military service: None

Political career: New York State Legislature, 1911–13

Assistant secretary of the navy, 1913–20

Governor of New York, 1929–33

Presidential annual salary: $75,000

Political party: Democrat

Died: 12 April 1945, Warm Springs, Georgia

Above: For just over 12 years, Franklin Roosevelt rewrote the political rule book. His unique achievement was not only his longevity in office; he was the architect of the modern presidency and his legacy has yet to be surpassed.

admiring the political career of his distant cousin, Theodore, but unlike the Republican Oyster Bay Roosevelts, the Hyde Park branch of the family were Democrats. Educated at Groton, an exclusive private school, he went on to Harvard. He dropped out of Columbia Law School, like Theodore before him, preferring to pursue a political career.

In 1905 he married Eleanor, Theodore Roosevelt's niece. They had six children, one of whom, a son named for his father, died in infancy. It was a turbulent relationship, but his wife would become one of Roosevelt's greatest political assets as well as an influential voice in US society in her own right.

Roosevelt was elected as a state senator in 1910, and three years later, following once more in his cousin's footsteps, he became assistant secretary to the navy in Woodrow Wilson's administration. In 1920, as a rising star

among Democrats, he was selected as the party's vice-presidential candidate. The example set by Theodore occurred to New York's party bosses, as the nomination for vice president would effectively remove a Roosevelt who had antagonized Tammany Hall from meddling in state politics. Defeated at the polls, he was temporarily out of the political limelight when, a year later, he was struck down with polio.

It was a long and painful recovery. Roosevelt regained partial use of his legs, but was largely confined to a wheelchair. The extent of his disability was kept from public knowledge in case it damaged his chances of returning to public office. In 1924, at the Democrat National Convention in Madison Square Garden, he gave the presidential nomination speech for the New York state governor, Al Smith. More relevant than his failure to influence the delegates, who selected John Davis from West Virginia instead, was the fact that he was able to walk a few steps to the podium, appearing his usual relaxed and confident self.

In 1928, Smith invited Roosevelt to give the nomination speech again, and as the party's presidential candidate he persuaded his fellow New Yorker to run for office as the state's governor. Smith lost to Hoover in the presidential election, but Roosevelt won an upset victory in New York. Four years later he became president and the Democrats gained control of Congress. He was 51 years old when he entered the White House: it was to be his home for the rest of his life.

THE NEW DEAL

Roosevelt was the outstanding politician of his generation. He understood that radio let him talk directly with the people. Moreover by making news he controlled the political agenda. Hoover had held one press conference a month during his last 12 months in office; Roosevelt averaged one a week during his 12 years in the presidency. He was aware of the importance of symbolic gestures: flying to the Democrat convention to make a speech accepting his nomination in 1932 was news because it was new. So too was his programme to aid national recovery, its name partly borrowed from his cousin's political lexicon: the New Deal.

Roosevelt's New Deal was introduced in a whirlwind of legislation during the frenzied activity of his first hundred days in office. It was initially aimed at bringing stability to the nation's financial system, devising a system of federal relief and job creation for the unemployed and reviving US capitalism. It was less a coherent plan than a way of giving effect to what he had referred to in a speech before he became president as "bold, persistent experimentation" to cure the ills of the Depression. He had back-up. His 'Brains Trust' was a group of intellectuals and

Below: Roosevelt convinced Americans that it was safe to reinvest their money in the nation's banks.

academic advisors who helped formulate the major legislative initiatives of the New Deal.

To stabilize the banking system, Roosevelt moved swiftly. After declaring a four-day bank holiday, he persuaded Congress to pass emergency legislation allowing them to open for business again only after their financial probity had been checked. His first 'fireside chat' on 12 March 1933 explained in simple terms the principles of banking to

Above: The construction of the Grand Coulee Dam was instigated under the presidency of Roosevelt, in a drive to end the Depression and provide employment.

his audience and persuaded them that it was safer to keep their money in a "reopened bank than under the mattress". The following day, queues formed outside banks to put back the cash that had been taken out in a panic. Roosevelt's was the voice of reassurance. Later in the year the Federal Reserve Board brought the banking system under tighter control.

The most controversial part of the New Deal, passed during the first hundred days, was the National Industrial Recovery Act. It established the Public Works Administration, a job creation agency, and the National Recovery Agency, which aimed to place the relationship between employers and their workforces on a more equitable basis. Unsurprisingly this generated opposition among industrial and business leaders. In 1935 the Supreme Court declared it unconstitutional.

Government involvement was seen as the key to economic regeneration, nowhere more so than in the Tennessee Valley Authority (TVA), set up in 1933. Roosevelt envisaged it as "a corporation

Above: Huey Long, US Senator, was a popular and charismatic radical who promoted the redistribution of wealth. He was assassinated in 1935.

clothed with the power of government but possessed of the flexibility and initiative of a private enterprise". Through major public works projects that provided employment in an area badly affected by the Depression, the TVA brought electricity to rural areas, encouraged new industries to come to the region and also worked to revive agricultural production.

As the economic recession in Europe deepened, demagogues assumed dictatorial power. In January 1933, a few weeks before Roosevelt was inaugurated, Adolf Hitler became chancellor of Germany. In Italy, Benito Mussolini had held office for a decade. The former governor of Louisiana, senator Huey Long, appealed to Americans with his radical populism and his call for a redistribution of the USA's wealth from rich to poor. Initially Long supported Roosevelt but the success of his 'Share our Wealth' organization, established in 1934, made him potentially a power-broker in national politics and fed his own presidential ambitions. In September 1935, Long was assassinated in the state capitol in Baton Rouge.

Re-elected in a landslide victory, Roosevelt's second administration was dominated by his attempt to 'pack' a recalcitrant Supreme Court with his supporters. The president proposed new legislation that would allow him to nominate an additional member for each justice over the age of 70, but the move was defeated in the Senate. It was a major political humiliation but it also left a lasting impression on the Supreme Court, which never again struck down New Deal legislation.

Roosevelt started to reform the executive branch of government to create 'the modern Presidency' with access to sources of information and power independent of the major departments of state represented in the Cabinet. The economy spluttered along. A civil war was fought in Spain. War broke out in Europe. The president ran for an unprecedented third term and once more won an easy victory.

AFTER PEARL HARBOR

World War II brought the Depression to an end. It revitalized the US economy as the United States became, in Roosevelt's words, "the great arsenal of democracy". After the Japanese attacked Pearl Harbor in 1941, US troops crossed the Atlantic to join the conflict in Europe and at the same time fought their way across the Pacific against Japan.

Their commander-in-chief, by now exhausted and ill, was re-elected for a fourth term in 1944. On 12 April 1945, just a few months after his inauguration, Franklin Roosevelt, whose place among the greatest of American presidents was assured, died in Warm Springs, Georgia, where more than 30 years previously he had convalesced from polio. He was 63 years old.

THE AMERICAN CENTURY

In February 1941, Henry Luce, the founder of *Time* and *Life* magazines, coined the phrase in an editorial. "The American Century" should be one in which the United States recognized that it had, in Franklin Roosevelt's words, "a rendezvous with destiny". Luce argued that the USA should be "the Good Samaritan of the entire world". Isolationism was no longer an option. To ensure the survival of democracy as a way of life, the United States should be prepared to take its place at the centre of the world stage.

ELEANOR ROOSEVELT

Eleanor Roosevelt was born in New York City in 1884. She married Franklin Roosevelt at the age of 20, and they had six children. Eleanor was the most high-profile first lady up to that time, and she became a political figure in her own right, speaking out on a variety of issues and travelling widely within the United States as well as overseas. After her husband died, she continued to be active in public life, at one time as a member of the USA's delegation to the United Nations. She died in 1962, aged 78.

Left: Eleanor Roosevelt proved to be a formidable first lady.

HOLLYWOOD
IN THE 1930s

The Jazz Singer (1927) revolutionized the film industry: it was the first feature-length movie to have synchronized sound. Movies now talked and their accent was American.

The 1930s were Hollywood's 'Golden Age': by the end of the decade, more than 500 films were being made each year. Numerous films that are still regarded as classics were produced and the studios created a host of enduring stars. As the USA's economic depression deepened, the Hollywood studios provided glamour and escapist entertainment for audiences who faced mounting challenges in their drab daily lives.

The five major studios – Warner Brothers, MGM, Paramount, RKO and 20th Century Fox – all used the so-called 'studio system'. This determined how the industry was organized: studios produced movies primarily on their own film-making lots, owned the distribution rights and even the theatres

Below: The epic production Gone With the Wind *became the highest grossing film of all time until the 1960s.*

in which their films were shown. At the same time, under the star system, the studios controlled the lives of the actors and actresses they placed under contract. Names were changed, biographies were re-written, and the stars reflected the image that the studio wanted to project. The contracts gave the actors little or no say in the choice of parts they played, and often included 'morality clauses' in an attempt to guard against adverse publicity.

Irving Thalberg, vice president of production at MGM, used the star system with outstanding success, fostering the careers of Greta Garbo, Joan Crawford, Jean Harlow, Clark Gable and Spencer Tracy among others. At other studios Katherine Hepburn, Marlene Dietrich, Cary Grant and Gary Cooper also became major stars.

The early 1930s produced classics of the gangster genre, such as *Little Caesar* (1930), *The Public Enemy* (1931) and *Scarface* (1932), with stars such as Edward G. Robinson and James Cagney. The Marx Brothers made comedies, and Charlie Chaplin directed the satire *Modern Times* in 1936. Fred Astaire had a screen test at RKO. His report read, "Losing hair. Can't sing. Balding. Can dance a little" – which he

Above: Shirley Temple presented a special Academy Award to Walt Disney for Snow White and the Seven Dwarfs *in 1939; it was one of the biggest ever box office hits.*

proceeded to do with Ginger Rogers throughout the decade. Other notable movies included Frank Capra's *It Happened One Night* (1934), which won five Oscars, and Walt Disney's first feature-length cartoon, *Snow White and the Seven Dwarfs* (1937). In 1939 *Stagecoach*, John Ford's revival of the Western with John Wayne as the Ringo Kid, was released, and Clark Gable starred with Vivien Leigh in *Gone with the Wind*.

Hollywood avoided the harsher realities of contemporary life. Out of the thousands of films made during the New Deal years, very few touched upon the Depression, or such contemporary European events as the Spanish Civil War and the advance of fascism in Italy and Germany.

In 1937 Warner Brothers gave an acting contract to a radio announcer from Illinois. Forty-three years later, Ronald Reagan, who believed in happy endings, landed his most important role: president of the United States.

PEARL HARBOR
1941

"Yesterday, December 7, 1941, a date which will live in infamy, the United States of America was suddenly and deliberately attacked by naval and air forces of the Empire of Japan." In response, President Roosevelt asked Congress to declare war.

Pearl Harbor on the Hawaiian island of O'ahu was then the headquarters of the US Pacific fleet, which in May 1940 had moved there from its San Diego base. By the time the Japanese air strikes had ended, eight of its ships had been crippled or sunk, three others were damaged, almost 200 aircraft had been destroyed, and close to 2,500 personnel had been killed. Bombers flying from

Below: During the Japanese attack, a small boat attempts to rescue survivors from the USS West Virginia.

Japanese aircraft carriers 320km (200 miles) away had taken the US forces by surprise.

JAPAN ATTACKS

It was Admiral Isoroku Yamamoto's idea. If the USA's naval presence in the Pacific could be neutralized by this one bold attack, Japan could launch an offensive against Hong Kong, Malaya, the Philippines and Guam, bringing it new bases and access to raw materials. Defences could be prepared against the inevitable counterattack. It was a high stakes gamble. The Japanese prime minister, General Hideki Tojo, observed: "Our Empire stands at the threshold of glory or oblivion."

On Sunday 7 December, the first wave of attacks came at just before eight in the morning, local time; 183 bombers

Above: More than half of those who died in the raid were on board the USS Arizona.

took part. The Japanese commander Mitsuo Fuchida's message back to the fleet – "Tora! Tora! Tora!" – signalled that the surprise was complete. The greatest explosion came as the forward magazine of the USS *Arizona* was hit. Almost one thousand members of its crew died. The raid took a little more than half an hour. There was a lull; then, 25 minutes later, the second wave of 167 bombers arrived. The major damage to the fleet had been done, but Pearl Harbor continued to be pounded for another hour before the Japanese broke off their attack. Even so, they left important potential targets, including fuel storage tanks, intact.

The Japanese had achieved a short-term tactical victory. Its strategic significance was predictable: the United States fought back. The attack turned public opinion from a position of isola-tionism to a recognition that the United States should enter the war. As Yamamoto later came to realize: "We have awakened a sleeping giant and have instilled in him a terrible resolve."

WORLD WAR II
1939–1945

On 11 December 1941, four days after Pearl Harbor, in accordance with the terms of their Axis pact with Japan, Germany and Italy declared war on the United States. Within two weeks, Winston Churchill, the British prime minister, had arrived in Washington. He urged Roosevelt to stand by the strategy agreed to earlier in the event that the United States was drawn into conflict with the Axis powers. Japan could wait. The war in Europe was the priority.

In January 1942, Roosevelt and Churchill settled on an Anglo-American invasion of Axis-held territory in North Africa. 'Operation Torch' began in November. Allied troops landed in

Above: Europe on the eve of World War II in 1939. War broke out when Germany invaded Poland.

THE AXIS PACT

In September 1940, Hitler, Mussolini and Saburo Kurusu, the Japanese ambassador in Berlin, signed the Axis pact, a tri-partite pact formalizing the military alliance between their three countries. It committed them "to assist one another if one of the Contracting Powers is attacked by a Power at present not involved in the European War or in the Japanese–Chinese conflict". In December 1941, Kurusu was in Washington when the Axis powers declared war on America.

Below: Mussolini and Hitler, the two European members of the Axis pact.

Morocco and Algeria and fought their way towards Tunisia. They met with some resistance from forces loyal to the Vichy government in France. German reinforcements fought to prevent the Allies linking up with the British Eighth Army, under the command of General Bernard Montgomery, which was moved east from Egypt after its victory at the Battle of El Alamein. Seven months later, Axis troops surrendered and the North African campaign came to an end.

On the eastern front, the year began with the Soviet forces lifting the German Siege of Leningrad, and ended with the Battle for Stalingrad. In December, Nazi atrocities against the Jews were denounced by the governments in Washington, London and Moscow. The perpetrators would be tried as war criminals.

Roosevelt became the first president to travel overseas during wartime, as well as the first to visit Africa, when he

met Churchill at the Casablanca Conference in January 1943. Joseph Stalin had been invited, but his concerns about the situation in Russia and misgivings over Allied strategy kept him at home. Roosevelt and Churchill agreed that the war would be fought until Germany surrendered unconditionally. They also planned the next invasion: Sicily. It took place on 10 July 1943. By September, Italy had surrendered. Earlier that year, Soviet troops had retaken Stalingrad and the tide of war on the eastern front began running against Germany. At the end of November, Roosevelt, Churchill and Stalin, the 'Big Three', met in Tehran and committed the Allies to the invasion of France.

Under General Eisenhower's command, 'Operation Overlord', also known as the Normandy landings, began on

6 June 1944. Two weeks later, there were more than half a million Allied troops in France. By August, Paris had been liberated. Allied armies fought their way towards Berlin. In February 1945, the 'Big Three' conferred at Yalta in the Crimea. With his armies advancing towards Germany, Stalin forced Churchill and Roosevelt, whose health was in terminal decline, to agree that Soviet troops would remain in occupied territory in Eastern Europe. When Roosevelt reported their discussions to Congress on 2 March, he remained seated: it was the first public acknowledgement of his disability. The following month he died, just 18 days before Hitler's suicide in Berlin. On 7 May Germany surrendered.

WAR IN THE PACIFIC

In the Pacific, the attack on Pearl Harbor had signalled the start of an offensive that, by the end of May 1942, had brought Japan territorial gains including the Philippines, Malaya, Burma, French Indo-China, the Dutch East Indies, Hong Kong and Singapore. On 4 June the Japanese and US navies faced each other at the Battle of Midway. America's decisive victory marked the beginning of the end. In August, the Allies started their first major offensive at Guadalcanal in the

---

THE VICHY GOVERNMENT

After Germany invaded France, Henri-Philippe Pétain's government, based in Vichy, controlled that part of it that remained unoccupied. Charles de Gaulle, leader of the Free French forces in exile, challenged its legitimacy. German troops marched into Vichy after the Allied invasion of North Africa. Following France's liberation, its leaders were tried as collaborators. Some were executed, though Pétain escaped that fate. De Gaulle commuted his sentence to life imprisonment. Pétain died in 1951.

Above: The largest seaborne invasion during World War II took place in Normandy in 1944 as the Allies invaded France.

Below: Roosevelt meets Churchill and Stalin at Yalta in the Crimea in February 1945; he died two months later.

Above: The iconic image of the Pacific War: Marines raise the US flag on Mount Suribachi, Iwo Jima.

Solomon Islands. It would be six more months before the Japanese withdrew from the island.

During 1943, a grim war of attrition took shape, forcing Japan gradually to relinquish control of its newly acquired territories. In June, Allied forces began the campaign to recover the islands in the Pacific. The Battle of Iwo Jima in February 1945 produced the most famous image of the Pacific War when, after fierce fighting, marines raised the US flag on Mount Suribachi. By the time war in Europe ended in May, the Japanese faced defeat. On 6 August an atomic bomb was dropped on Hiroshima, followed by another, three days later, on Nagasaki. The broadcast by the Japanese emperor on 15 August, the first time his voice had been heard in public, announced the surrender. It was over.

Below: The War in the Pacific continued after the conflict in Europe ended.

Below: The Battle of Midway significantly weakened Japan's military capacity.

AMERICAN CAMPAIGNS OF WORLD WAR II

1942
7 May: Battle of the Coral Sea
3 June: Battle of Midway
7 August: Guadalcanal
17 August: First USAAF raid in Europe
15 September: Papua New Guinea campaign
8 November: Operation Torch
1943
4 January: Tunisian campaign
2 March: Battle of the Bismarck Sea
30 June: South Pacific offensive
15 August: Aleutians retaken
17 August: Patton conquers Sicily
9 September: US army lands at Salerno, Italy
9 October: Schweinfurt raid
20 November: Central Pacific campaign begins
1944
22 January: Allies land at Anzio, Italy
7 February: Marshall Islands taken
4 June: Rome liberated
6 June: D-Day (Operation Overlord begins in Europe)
19 June: Battle of the Philippine Sea
15 August: Allied invasion of France
10 September: France liberated
11 September: Invasion of Germany
23 October: Battle of Leyte Gulf
24 November: Bombing of Japan begins
16 December: Battle of the Bulge
1945
9 January: Philippines Luzon campaign
8 February: Rhineland campaign
23 February: Battle of Iwo Jima
9 March: USAAF Tokyo raid
1 April: Okinawa campaign
2 May: Fall of Berlin
8 May: VE Day (Germany surrenders)
6 August: Atomic bomb dropped on Hiroshima
2 September: VJ Day (Japan surrenders)

THE INVENTION OF THE ATOMIC BOMB
1941–1945

Albert Einstein wrote to Franklin Roosevelt on 2 August 1939. The most famous physicist in the world, who had escaped from Nazi antisemitism to come to Princeton University, had a warning for the president: "It may become possible to set up a nuclear chain reaction in a large mass of uranium." If this happened, he said, "extremely powerful bombs of a new type may thus be constructed". German scientists might already be working on such a device. Roosevelt ordered a programme of research and development that would culminate in the 'Manhattan Project'.

It was Robert Oppenheimer who took charge of the bomb's design at a laboratory at Los Alamos in the remote mountains of New Mexico. Enriched uranium was produced at Oak Ridge in Tennessee. In 1943, work began at Hanford in Washington State to construct a facility to make plutonium. By early 1945, scientists had enough enriched uranium and plutonium for their purposes.

Below: Truman's decision to drop atomic bombs on Japan ended the war, heralding the dawn of the nuclear age.

On 16 July a plutonium bomb was tested. It worked. As the mushroom cloud rose over the New Mexico desert, Oppenheimer recalled that the explosion brought to his mind a line from the *Bhagavad-Gita*, the Hindu scripture: "Now I am become Death, the destroyer of worlds."

LITTLE BOY AND FAT MAN
The decision to use the bomb was President Truman's. He had been unaware of the Manhattan Project's progress until he took office in April 1945. On 25 July, after informing Stalin of the successful test, news of which spies had already reported to the Soviet leader, Truman authorized its use against the Japanese.

Hiroshima was first. The *Enola Gay*, the bomber piloted by Colonel Paul

Above: Almost a quarter of a million people perished immediately or in the aftermath of the explosions.

Tibbets, dropped a uranium bomb, 'Little Boy', obliterating the city. 'Fat Man', the plutonium bomb, which exploded over Nagasaki, brought similar destruction. Those closest to the detonations were incinerated. Others who survived the initial blast died later from the effects of radiation.

Many scientists who worked on the Manhattan Project regretted developing a weapon of mass destruction. Politicians – none more so than the president of the United States, whose finger has hovered over the nuclear button at times of extreme international tension – have had to have the calm judgement and self-restraint not to use it again.

THE UNITED NATIONS

1944–1945

Even before the United States entered the war, its president looked forward to the peace. In August 1941, Roosevelt and Churchill met on ships of their respective navies in Placentia Bay, Newfoundland. One outcome of their discussions was the Atlantic Charter, issued on 14 August, establishing "certain common principles in the national policies of their respective countries on which they base their hopes for a better future for the world". These included an end to imperial ambitions, international economic co-operation and a "permanent system of general security" based on disarmament.

On 1 January 1942, 24 countries joined the United States and Britain in agreeing to subscribe to the Charter's provisions. They were convinced "that complete victory over their enemies is essential to defend life, liberty, independence and religious freedom, and to preserve human rights and justice in their own lands as well as in other lands". Roosevelt had proposed the collective term embodied in the statement's title and used for the first time: it was a "Declaration by the United Nations".

In November 1943, a Senate resolution, introduced by Tom Connally, chair of its Foreign Relations Committee, which had been framed in the office of the then junior senator from Missouri, Harry Truman, was approved. It recognized "the necessity of there being established at the earliest practicable date a general international organization, based on the principle of the sovereign equality of all peace-loving states, and open to membership by all such states, large and small, for the maintenance of international peace and security". The United States was thus committed to play a leading role in creating the United Nations.

A NEW CHARTER

Representatives from America, Britain, the Soviet Union and China met at Dumbarton Oaks, a mansion in Washington, from August to October 1944 and drew up proposals for "an international organization under the title of The United Nations", the membership of which was "open to all

Below: Fifty-one countries signed up to the charter to become the original members of the United Nations.

Above: The United Nations works to resolve international confrontations and to promote peace.

peace-loving states". The following year, 50 countries sent delegations to San Francisco to draw up its charter at a conference that opened on 25 April. The proceedings attracted media interest from around the world. One correspondent from Hearst's *Chicago World Herald and Tribune* observed them and became pessimistic about the organization's chances of success: his name was John F. Kennedy.

A COALITION FOR PEACE
The principal purpose, it was agreed, was "to maintain international peace and security". Unlike the League of Nations, the United Nations would be able to call on member states to give military support to its peacekeeping efforts. Through its General Assembly and Security Council it provided the mechanisms for the potential arbitration and resolution of international conflicts, although agreement would prove difficult as the post-war world became divided along the ideological fault lines of the Cold War.

Right: Though the United Nations building is situated in New York, the land it stands on is considered international territory.

On 26 June 1945, China became the first country to sign the Charter of the United Nations, followed by representatives from the other 49 nations. A State Department official, Alger Hiss, flew to Washington the next day and delivered the Charter to the White House. It was to come into force once it had been ratified by the governments of the nations comprising the permanent members of the Security Council – the United States, Britain, France, China and Russia – together with a majority of the other signatories. While this process took place, Poland also signed, to join as an original member of the organization. On 24 October, just over two months after the war ended, the United Nations was established. In December, Congress unanimously invited it to base its headquarters in the United States, and the following February the General Assembly agreed on New York as its permanent home.

ISRAEL AND PALESTINE
In 1947 the United Nations inherited one of its most intractable issues. Britain announced that it would terminate the mandate under which it had administered Palestine and asked the United Nations to decide the future government of that country. On 29 November the recommendations of the Special Committee on Palestine were accepted and the UN proposed the partition of the area into a Jewish state and an Arab state, with Jerusalem becoming an international zone. The compromise proved to be unworkable.

On 14 May the British mandate was relinquished, the State of Israel was proclaimed and fighting broke out. The Palestinian question, and the broader issues of Middle Eastern politics, would become continuing preoccupations not only for the United Nations but also for successive presidents of the United States government.

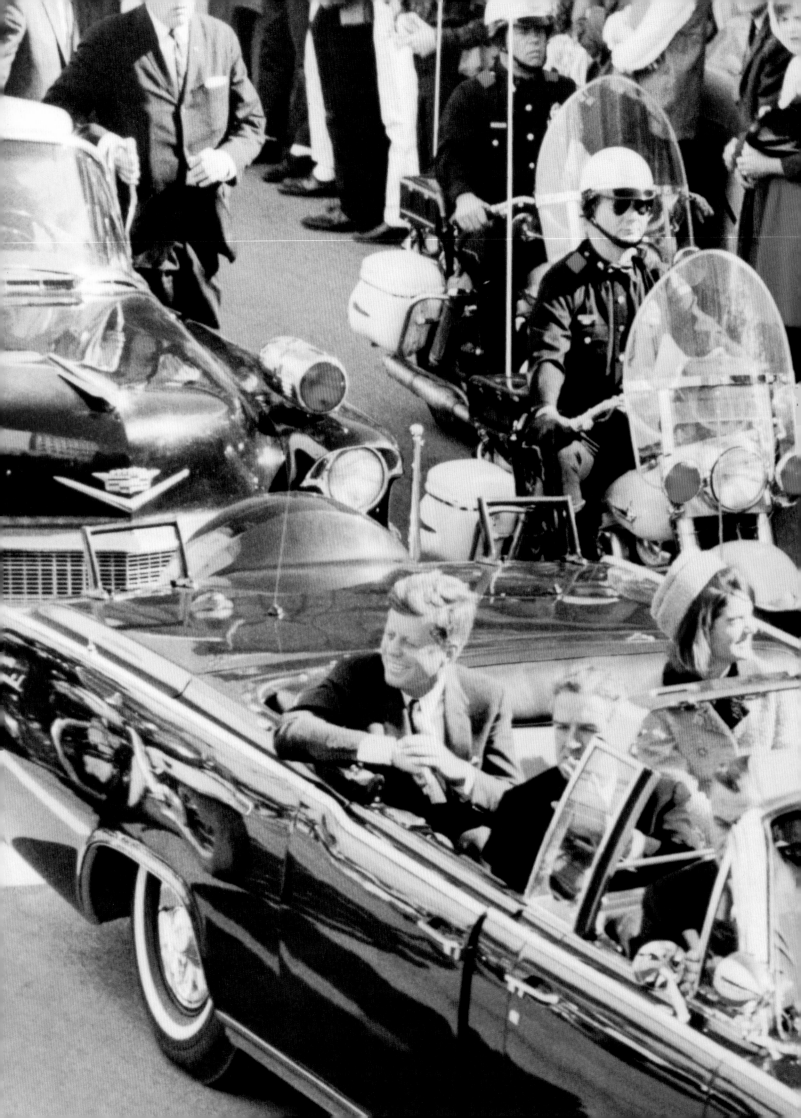

CHAPTER THREE

HARRY TRUMAN TO JOHN F. KENNEDY

1945–1963

Americans hated communism and feared nuclear war. Their reaction to the knowledge that communists had atomic weapons was predictable. Soon after World War II ended, the former allies became ideological enemies. In 1947, a former presidential advisor, Bernard Baruch, observed that: "We are today in the midst of a cold war." The phrase stuck. The battle lines in a new conflict of ideas, competing economic systems and political organization were drawn. In August 1949 the Soviet Union tested an atomic bomb. During the following year communists took control in China. With its enemies now led by dictators such as Joseph Stalin and Mao Tse Tung, how might the United States respond? Anxious Americans looked to their president for leadership. The Cold War broke out into open conflict in Korea, and the United States began its involvement in the quagmire of Vietnam.

Left: John F. Kennedy's open-top presidential limousine nears the Book Depository in Dallas, Texas.

HARRY TRUMAN
1945–1953

The sign on his desk said 'The buck stops here', a saying borrowed from his favourite pastime: poker. Harry Truman dealt the cards and played the USA's hand in the high-stakes game of post-war international politics. The only commander-in-chief to have seen active service in World War I, as president he fought once more for his belief that the United States should keep the world safe for democracy in its confrontation with communism. Stepping from the shadow of Roosevelt was a challenge in itself, but Truman understood the meaning of presidential power and accepted its responsibilities.

He was born in 1884 in Missouri. A protective mother, weak eyesight and studious inclinations set him apart from his contemporaries in the town of Independence. His one-time inclination to become a concert pianist was replaced by an ambition to have a military

Above: Truman's presidency encompassed the end of World War II and the beginning of the Cold War as the United States became a 'superpower'.

career, but he ended up working on the family farm. In 1905 he joined the National Guard. He went to France in World War I, becoming a captain in the artillery. In 1919 he married Bess Wallace, and their only daughter, Margaret, was born in 1924.

Politics provided an escape route for Truman from his failed haberdashery

business. In 1922, supported by Tom Pendergast's Kansas City Democrat machine, Truman was elected as a district judge. He remained a local politician until in 1934 he was elected to the federal Senate. When the United States entered the war, Truman headed a committee investigating waste in defence appropriations and spending. In 1944 he emerged as the compromise candidate for the vice presidency. He had been in his job for only 82 days when Roosevelt died.

ATOMIC BOMB

"We have discovered the most terrible bomb in the history of the world," Truman confided to his diary on 25 July 1945. That day, at the Potsdam conference, he had told Stalin the news. On 1 August the Potsdam Declaration made it clear that the Allied leaders expected the Japanese to agree to an unconditional surrender or else "the alternative for Japan is prompt and utter

Below: Truman's first administration was marked by industrial unrest in part due to Congress's anti-union legislation.

Born: 8 May 1884, Lamar, Missouri
Parents: John (1851–1914) and Martha (1852–1947)
Family background: Farming
Education: University of Kansas City Law School (did not graduate)
Religion: Baptist
Occupation: Farmer, public service
Military service: Colonel, US Army, World War I
Political career: Judge: Jackson County Court, 1922–4
Presiding judge: Jackson County Court, 1926–34
US Senate, 1935–45
Vice president, 1945
Presidential annual salary: $75,000, increased to $100,000 + $50,000 expenses (1949)
Political party: Democrat
Died: 26 December 1972, Kansas City, Missouri

THE MARSHALL PLAN

On 5 June 1947, a speech given at Harvard University by George C. Marshall, Truman's secretary of state, invited European governments to co-operate in planning the distribution of $20 billion of US aid. The Marshall Plan was eagerly embraced in western Europe, but rejected by the Soviet Union and the countries it dominated in the east. Congress approved the plan the following year and US dollars began to flow across the Atlantic, laying the foundations for the creation of the European Economic Community.

destruction". Atomic explosions ended the war and detonated the way to a high-risk future in the nuclear age.

At home, the transition to a peacetime economy took place against a background of industrial unrest. Truman asked Congress for powers to draft striking workers into the military in an emergency. It cost him electoral support. In 1946, the Democrats lost control of Congress. The following year, the legislature, overturning Truman's veto, passed the Taft-Hartley Act, restricting the activity of the unions.

Abroad, the Truman Doctrine (see next page) saw a world divided into those prepared to defend democracy and those who sought to undermine it.

On 26 July 1947, Congress, which shared the president's concern about the threat from communism, passed the National Security Act, establishing the National Security Council, the Central Intelligence Agency and re-naming the Department of War the Department of Defense. The following year, it approved the European Recovery Programme – the Marshall Plan – to provide aid to that part of Europe that had not disappeared behind the 'Iron Curtain'.

On election night 1948, the *Chicago Herald Tribune* had as its front page headline "Dewey Defeats Truman". He did not. In an upset victory, Truman was re-elected and the Democrats regained control of Congress. In his inaugural address in 1949, the president suggested that it was "the beginning not only of a new administration, but of a period that will be eventful for us and for the world". So it proved.

The Soviet Union acquired nuclear weapons. The communist People's Republic of China was proclaimed. The United States began to develop the hydrogen bomb. Senator Joseph McCarthy embarked on his crusade against communism within the United States. Mao and Stalin became allies. In June 1950, North Korea invaded South Korea. US forces, under the auspices of

Above: The United States provided most of the troops from 16 member countries sent to fight in Korea under a United Nations Joint Command.

the United Nations, fought an increasingly unpopular war in South-east Asia. In 1952, when a strike threatened steel production for the war effort, the president ordered the federal government to take over the mills, an action later declared unconstitutional.

Truman retired to Independence, his home town in Missouri, to write his memoirs. He was resigned, he said, to his administration being "cussed and discussed for years to come". Harry Truman died on 26 December 1972.

BESS TRUMAN

Elizabeth 'Bess' Wallace was born in Independence, Missouri, in 1885. She went to school with Harry Truman. In 1919, she married him. Five years later, their daughter, Mary Margaret, was born. After the high-profile public life of her predecessor, Eleanor Roosevelt, Bess Truman was a more traditional first lady, leaving politics to her husband while she pursued charity work. She died in 1982 at the age of 97: the longest-living first lady.

THE 'IRON CURTAIN'

Winston Churchill coined the vivid expression that described the post-war ideological division in Europe: "From Stettin in the Baltic to Trieste in the Adriatic, an iron curtain has descended across the Continent." He called on the western democracies to unite in the face of the communist challenge, emphasizing the 'special relationship' between Britain and the United States: the cornerstone of contemporary British foreign policy.

THE TRUMAN DOCTRINE
1947

After World War II, the British Empire was bankrupt. It could not maintain its military presence overseas, even close to home. In February 1947, its Labour government, having already retreated from India, Burma and the Middle East, decided to withdraw its forces from Greece and Turkey. Would Americans be persuaded to fill the international power vacuum? If they did not, what would be the outcome?

The previous year, George Kennan, then a senior US diplomat in Moscow, had sent his 'long telegram' to the State Department outlining what he saw as the Soviet Union's intentions. Once it was decided on a course of action the Soviet government was "like a persistent toy automobile wound up and headed in a given direction, stopping only when it meets with some unanswerable force. In these circumstances it is clear that the main element of any United States policy toward the Soviet Union

Below: During the Cold War, the Pentagon, built in 1941, became the command centre of the American military.

must be that of long-term, patient but firm and vigilant containment of Russian expansive tendencies." The United States had to stand up and be counted. There could be no retreat into isolationism.

This was the president's message to Congress on 12 March 1947, requesting $400 million for aid to Greece and Turkey, which became known as the 'Truman Doctrine'. Like President Monroe's Doctrine, adopted over a century earlier, it defined the terms of

Above: Harry Truman and Joseph Stalin at the Potsdam conference. Soon after, war-time allies became ideological enemies and the Cold War began.

US foreign policy. It aimed to contain what it saw as an aggressively expansionist ideology. Nations had to "choose between alternative ways of life": either democracy or a system that "relies upon terror and oppression, a controlled press and radio; fixed elections and the suppression of personal freedom".

Truman argued that "it must be the policy of the United States to support free peoples who are resisting attempted subjugation by armed minorities or by outside pressures". Congress agreed. In 1950, a National Security Council Report (NSC 68) recommended the development of "a level of military readiness which can be maintained as long as necessary as a deterrent to Soviet aggression" and that "the internal security of the United States against dangers of sabotage, subversion and espionage" be assured.

The Cold War was "a real war in which the survival of the free world is at stake". Its architecture had been constructed within three years of the meeting between Truman and Stalin as wartime allies in Potsdam.

THE POWER OF TELEVISION

On 4 September 1951, President Truman was in San Francisco. His speech opening the conference that concluded the Peace Treaty with Japan was seen on television, in the first nationwide broadcast in US history. Truman was already familiar with the new medium. In October 1947 he had made the first televised address from the White House. By the time of his West Coast broadcast, there were 13 million television sets in the United States. Two years later, half the nation's population had a set.

In 1952, Dwight Eisenhower's presidential campaign televised a series of political advertisements. They were called 'Eisenhower Answers America'. However, the most famous broadcast of the campaign came from his vice-presidential candidate, Richard Nixon, who had been accused by the press of having a 'secret fund' donated by wealthy backers. Before an audience estimated at 60 million people, he revealed details of his financial affairs and told the tale of a gift his family had received: "A little cocker spaniel dog, and our little girl Tricia, the six-year-old, named it Checkers. And you know, the kid, like all kids, loved the dog, and regardless of what they say about it, we are going to keep it." The overwhelmingly positive public reaction to the 'Checkers Speech' meant that Nixon kept his place on the ticket as well. The response also convinced him of the value of appealing directly to the people. He believed he could use television to his advantage, until he came up against an even better performer: John F. Kennedy.

Television's power to influence its audience was confirmed when Edward R. Murrow, the highly respected CBS correspondent, made a documentary about the 'Red Scare' that helped to turn public opinion against Senator

Joseph McCarthy's anti-communist witch-hunt. In 1957, Murrow observed that in the television age, neither Jefferson nor Lincoln could have become president: "Jefferson had a most abrasive voice and did not suffer fools gladly. Mr Lincoln did not move gracefully, was not a handsome man, had a wife who was not a political asset and was a solitary man." From the 1950s onwards, Americans who had previously only heard their presidents on radio now became used to seeing them on television. This brought a new style to presidential politics, placing a premium

Above: President Truman quickly became aware of the persuasive power of television. From this time on image became all-important.

on both appearance and performance. It was John F. Kennedy who symbolized the change. He looked good on television and this was believed to have given him the decisive edge when he debated with Nixon during the 1960 campaign. Television became the dominant medium of political communication as the drama of the presidency was played out in homes across the United States.

Left: California senator Richard M. Nixon speaks to the nation on a coast-to-coast radio-television hook-up. The senator, who was at the time the Republican vice-presidential candidate, addressed the American people from Los Angeles in an attempt to explain fully his controversial $18,000 expense fund. His political future was expected to hang on the reception of this one dramatic speech.

THE KOREAN WAR
1950–1953

Korea had been occupied by Japan during World War II, and after the war it was left a divided country. Following the Japanese surrender, the Soviet Union took control of the north of the country and the United States the south, with the border fixed along the 38th parallel. Despite the promise of reunification, by 1948 two separate states were established: the Northern Democratic People's Republic of Korea, headed by Kim Il-sung, and the Southern Republic of Korea, led by Syngman Rhee. The north was under the protection of Soviet Russia and the south by the United States. On 25 June 1950, North Korea invaded the South in an attempt to re-unify the country by military force. The south were caught off guard, despite rumours of impending North Korean action.

The United Nations immediately called for North Korea to withdraw its forces. Four days later, the South Korean capital of Seoul had been occupied. On 30 June President Truman committed

US troops to intervene to enforce the United Nations resolution demanding a cessation of hostilities. The president chose not to ask Congress for a declaration of war because technically he was acting to fulfil the USA's obligation to assist in a United Nations mission to restore peace.

The United Nations command was established under General Douglas MacArthur. Its troops were initially forced into retreat, but on 15 September they mounted a successful counter-attack with an amphibious landing at Inchon, behind North Korean lines, fighting their way back up the Korean peninsula. By the end of the month, they had recaptured the territory up to the 38th parallel.

Truman then agreed to MacArthur's proposal to invade the North, potentially transforming the United Nations 'police action' into what could be seen as a war of national liberation. He did so on the understanding that should the Soviet Union or China intervene on

Above: United Nations forces parachute into the Korean War. The USA supplied the greatest number of combat troops.

North Korea's side, risking escalation to a wider – and possibly a nuclear – war, then the Americans should stop their advance. MacArthur ignored Truman's proviso. Despite a warning from the Chinese foreign minister Chou En-Lai that his country would intervene if United States forces crossed the 38th parallel, he started moving US troops to the Yalu River.

The Chinese remained true to their word. In November, the Chinese People's Volunteer Army, with some military aid from the Soviets, entered the war, forcing the Americans into a hasty retreat from the Chosin Reservoir.

In early January 1951 Seoul was abandoned once more, and by the end of the month China's forces had advanced further south before being once again pushed back. By March, Seoul was once more under the control of the United Nations, but the conflict had developed into a stalemate that, despite diplomatic efforts, seemed incapable of resolution.

Below: The Korean peninsula was divided between the communist North and the non-communist South.

Below: Despite advances in battle tactics gained in World War II, the Korean War battles were based on trench warfare.

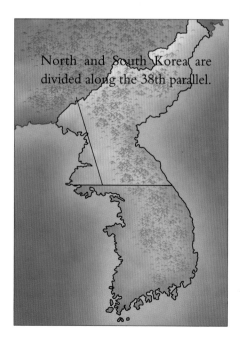

North and South Korea are divided along the 38th parallel.

Above: The 38th parallel became the line marking the demilitarized zone and the border between North and South Korea.

In the fevered atmosphere that accompanied the Chinese intervention, Truman's remarks at a press conference had been interpreted to suggest that the United States was contemplating using atomic bombs to end the conflict. It was not the case, but General MacArthur would have been happy to exercise the nuclear option. The morale of the retreating US forces was low, and a war of containment was indecisive: for MacArthur there was "no substitute for victory". His campaign against Truman's conduct of the Korean conflict, fought in private and in public, amounted to insubordination: challenging a basic principle of the USA's republican government, that a civilian commander-in-chief – the president – should control the military. On 12 April 1951, Truman fired him.

There was a public outcry in support of MacArthur. On his triumphant return to the United States (for the first time in 20 years), he was welcomed with a ticker-tape parade in New York that was twice the size of that which had greeted Eisenhower when he had arrived back from Europe in 1945, demonstrating that his celebrity could temporarily eclipse his lack of political judgement. However, there were few who supported his demand to escalate the war against China. Instead, lacking an obvious exit strategy, the United States became resigned to a lengthy military commitment in Korea.

In 1952, Eisenhower was elected to the presidency not least because of his promise to end the war in Korea. In November, as president elect, he travelled to Korea to inject new life into the peace negotiations. An armistice was signed in July 1953. A demilitarized zone – which remains in place today – was established around the 38th parallel, and the two separate nations continued to maintain an uneasy peace.

Estimates of the human costs of the war vary: of 150,000 US casualties, approximately 34,000 were killed in action. The Chinese suffered in the region of 900,000 casualties and the Korean dead and wounded may have been as high as two million. The lessons from the Korean War had been all but forgotten when in the following decade the United States intervened militarily in another war in a divided country in South-east Asia: Vietnam.

Below: Truman sacked MacArthur, but he returned home from Korea to a hero's reception.

DWIGHT EISENHOWER
1953–1961

The first Republican president since Ulysses S. Grant to serve two full terms in the White House was Dwight Eisenhower, a trusted war hero. No 20th-century commander-in-chief had more military experience than the former supreme commander of Allied forces in Europe during World War II. The reassuring image projected by the president did much to shape nostalgic memories of his time in office. Americans elected Eisenhower to the White House because he made them feel safe.

Born in Texas in 1890, Eisenhower grew up in Kansas. Despite his mother's pacifism, in 1911 he entered the military academy at West Point, graduating in 1915 and marrying Mamie Doud the following year. During World War I he trained tank crews in Pennsylvania. Following studies at the army's Staff College at Fort Leavenworth in Kansas, he became an aide to General Pershing and then to General MacArthur. In Washington, shortly after the attack on Pearl Harbor, Eisenhower's capacity for

Born: 14 October 1890, Denison, Texas
Parents: David (1863–1942) and Ida (1862–1946)
Family background: Engineering
Education: US Military Academy, West Point (1915)
Religion: Presbyterian
Occupation: Soldier
Military service: Supreme Allied commander (Europe), World War II General of the army
Political career: None
Presidential annual salary: $100,000 + $50,000 expenses
Political party: Republican
Died: 28 March 1969, Washington DC

strategic thinking and military planning impressed the army chief of staff, George Marshall.

From 1942 onwards, as the United States entered World War II, Eisenhower took charge of the Allied invasions of North Africa, Sicily and Italy, followed in 1944 by the Normandy landings of Operation Overlord. He returned to the USA as army chief of staff.

In 1948 he left the military to become president of Columbia University in New York. He then spent another two years in Europe as supreme commander of the North Atlantic Treaty Organisation (NATO). Both Democrats and Republicans courted him as a potential presidential candidate. In 1952, he defeated Robert Taft,

Above: Eisenhower, already a military hero, regained the presidency for the Republicans after an interval of 20 years.

'Mr Republican' and son of the former president, to win the party's nomination and then the White House.

A NEW PHASE OF INTERNATIONAL RELATIONS

Less than two months after Eisenhower took office, Stalin died. US relations with the Soviet Union entered a new phase when Nikita Khrushchev established himself as its undisputed leader. The USA's fear of communism at home and abroad remained. In 1951, the atmosphere of the times was dramatized in the high-profile trial of Ethel and

She was born Mamie Doud in Iowa in 1896 and grew up in Colorado and Texas, where she met Dwight Eisenhower, who was then a second lieutenant at Fort Sam Houston. They married in 1916. They had two sons: their first succumbed to scarlet fever at the age of four, and their second followed his father into the army and later became US ambassador to Belgium. Mamie was a popular first lady, using her experience as an army officer's wife to good effect when she had to organize the frequent social gatherings at the White House. She died in 1979 and was buried alongside her husband in Abilene, Kansas.

Above: Eisenhower and Nikita Khrushchev in 1955 at the first Cold War summit meeting between US and Soviet leaders.

Below: The Rosenbergs, members of the American Communist party, were found guilty of treason and executed for passing state secrets to the Soviets.

Julius Rosenberg who were found guilty of passing atomic secrets to the Soviets. They received the death penalty but the trial and conviction caused controversy. In June 1953 Eisenhower

Below: Federal troops escort black pupils to school in Arkansas. The state refused to accept the Supreme Court's desegregation ruling.

refused Ethel's last-minute clemency plea and she was executed on the same day as her husband; they were the only two US civilians to be executed for espionage during the Cold War.

In October 1953, the president announced a 'New Look' defence and national security policy, which made it clear that, "In the event of hostilities, the United States will consider nuclear weapons to be as available for use as other munitions." The threat of massive

retaliation using atomic bombs would be the basis of Eisenhower's strategy to keep the peace.

When North Vietnamese communist forces won the battle of Dien Bien Phu in 1954, ending France's hope of re-establishing its empire in Indo-China, Eisenhower explained the implications of the defeat: "You have a row of dominoes set up, you knock over the first one, and what will happen to the last one is the certainty that it will go over very quickly." US aid to South Vietnam was increased to try to stop communist expansion and the toppling of more dominoes. Although Eisenhower did not commit US troops to Vietnam in any great numbers, his 'domino theory' became part of the strategic thinking that eventually drew the United States inexorably into the Vietnam War.

STATES ENTERING THE UNION DURING EISENHOWER'S PRESIDENCY:

ALASKA

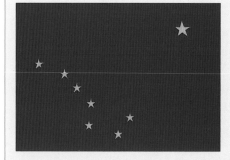

Entered the Union: 1959
Pre-state history: Land bought from Russia (1867); organized as Alaska Territory (1912)
Total population in 1960 census: 223,866
Electoral College votes in 1960: 3

HAWAII

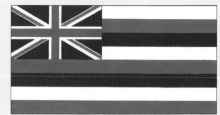

Entered the Union: 1959
Pre-state history: Republic of Hawaii (1894); annexed by US and organized as Hawaii Territory (1898)
Total population in 1960 census: 632,772
Electoral College votes in 1960: 3

DEEPENING CRISES

In July 1955, Eisenhower had a meeting with Khrushchev in Geneva. As Cold War tensions temporarily eased, the president's prestige was high and he contemplated running for re-election. In September, he had a heart attack, but he recovered and went on to win a second term. In the midst of the election, British and French troops seized the Suez Canal after Egypt had nationalized and then closed it. Soviet tanks moved into Hungary and crushed the national uprising against the country's communist government. Eisenhower's refusal to support the USA's European allies forced them to withdraw from Suez, and his decision not to intervene behind the Iron Curtain meant that the Soviet Union remained in control of Hungary. After these two crises, and in response to the threat of the further expansion of Soviet influence, particularly in the Middle East, the 'Eisenhower Doctrine' committed the United States military to protect that region against "overt aggression from International Communism".

His second term ended amid criticisms of complacency. When Russia launched Sputnik, the artificial satellite led to doubts about the USA's lead over the Soviet Union in missile technology. As well as rising international tensions, the Civil Rights movement gained momentum, increasing difficulties on the domestic front. The president had to send federal troops to Little Rock, Arkansas, to force its racially segregated high school to admit nine black students who had legally enrolled there in 1957. In 1960 his Paris summit with Khrushchev collapsed after revelations that an American U-2 spy plane had been shot down over the Soviet Union.

At the end of his term of office Eisenhower retired to his farm at Gettysburg. He died in 1969. His last words expressed a wish and a command: "I want to go; God take me."

Left: Eisenhower supported the construction of the interstate highway system leading to major improvements in the USA's transportation network.

BROWN v. BOARD OF EDUCATION
1954

Thurgood Marshall was an African-American descended from slaves, whose interest in the law derived from being made to read the Constitution as a school punishment. As chief counsel for the National Association for the Advancement of Colored People (NAACP) he argued a landmark case known as Brown v. Board of Education of Topeka before the Supreme Court.

In the class action the named plaintiff, Oliver Brown, was one of 13 parents who set out to challenge the 'separate but equal' policy under which schools in Southern states were segregated, arguing that the result was not equal but inferior education for black students. In 1954, the Supreme Court reached its decision, paving the way for desegregation in the South. Earl Warren, a former Republican governor of California, and appointed chief justice by President Eisenhower, made sure the Court's decision on the case was

Below: Thurgood Marshall (centre), with George Hayes (left) and James Nabrit (right), the lawyers who argued the case for school desegregation.

unanimous, and between them Marshall and Warren helped advance the cause of civil rights. The ruling was that the school system that had existed in the South since the end of the Civil War was unconstitutional, opening the way for the dismantling of 'Jim Crow' laws and the end of racial segregation.

After the end of World War II, despite violence and intimidation, Southern blacks began to take legal action against the self-evidently inferior facilities in which their children were educated. Overcrowded, poorly constructed, a long way from the neighbourhoods in which they lived, with no transportation to them, black schools did not compare to those that whites attended. In 1951, a South Carolina judge, Julius Waring, in a dissenting opinion in the case of Briggs v. Elliot, had argued that "segregation in education can never produce equality". It was this case and others like it that paved the way for the Supreme Court to make its ruling.

Marshall put the case against 'Jim Crow' laws. If individual states had the power to deny the Fourteenth Amendment, which prohibited them from

'JIM CROW'

The expression 'Jim Crow' derives from a song and dance routine, 'Jump Jim Crow', that was performed in blackface by a white comedian, 'Daddy' Rice, in the 1830s. By the Civil War, it had become one of the many pejorative and racist epithets used by white Americans to describe black people. Later it came to be associated with the Southern laws that ensured black people were deprived of their civil and political rights. Strict segregation was enforced not only by state laws, supported by Supreme Court decisions and federal government inaction, but also by the constant threat and use of violence.

passing and enforcing "any law which shall abridge the privileges or immunities of citizens of the United States", then, as he pointed out, "like the old Confederation, the Union becomes a mere rope of sand".

Warren's opinion, given additional force by the Court's complete agreement with him, relied on psychological and social scientific research suggesting that segregated education in itself induced a feeling of inferiority among black children. The Court shaped the law by not relying on precedent or analysis of the historical intent behind the Fourteenth Amendment.

The decision was not universally accepted. In Virginia, for example, the 'Massive Resistance' campaign against integration had state support that had to be fought in the federal courts.

The Warren Supreme Court made several other important decisions advancing the cause of civil liberties. In 1967, Warren was still chief justice when the first black American was appointed to it: Thurgood Marshall.

THE THREAT OF COMMUNISM

In February 1950, during a speech in Wheeling, West Virginia, Senator Joseph McCarthy from Wisconsin confronted his audience with a list of 205 communists whom he alleged were "shaping the policy of the State Department". The previous month, a prominent State Department official, Alger Hiss, had been convicted of perjury. He was sentenced to five years in prison. In his appearance before the House Un-American Activities Committee (HUAC), he had denied allegations that he was a communist. The case had brought national attention to Richard Nixon, the Committee member who

Right: McCarthy's dramatic denunciations of communists created a climate of fear throughout the United States.

pursued the accusation most aggressively. Truman's secretary of state, Dean Acheson, refused to condemn Hiss, using a biblical analogy: this was the final straw for McCarthy. His speech reserved its greatest invective for Acheson: "When this pompous diplomat in striped pants, with a phoney British accent, proclaimed to the American people that Christ on the Mount endorsed communism, high treason, and betrayal of a sacred trust,

THE HOUSE UN-AMERICAN ACTIVITIES COMMITTEE (HUAC)

HUAC was established in 1937 to investigate subversive activities by American extremists at both ends of the ideological spectrum. After World War II it concentrated on the perceived communist threat, launching its investigation of Hollywood and pursuing the case against Alger Hiss. HUAC operated independently of McCarthy's Senate committee but was equally zealous in its pursuit of communists, either real or imagined.

Below: The House Un-American Activities Committee investigated communist infiltration into all areas of public life.

the blasphemy was so great that it awakened the dormant indignation of the American people." Joseph McCarthy's anti-communist crusade was up and running.

McCarthy launched his investigations as chair of the Senate Committee on Government Operations, whereas HUAC was a committee set up by the House of Representatives. Three years previously, it had investigated communist activity in Hollywood. Some of those it called to testify, who refused to answer the question: "Are you now or have you ever been a member of the Communist party?" had been jailed for contempt, despite the fact that their right to silence was enshrined in the Fifth Amendment to the Constitution. 'Friendly' witnesses such as Walt Disney, Gary Cooper and the then president of the Screen Actors Guild, Ronald Reagan, expressed their concerns about communist influence in the industry. In 1951, a second round of hearings, influenced by the hysteria whipped up by McCarthy, resulted in the 'naming of names'. Hollywood's blacklist of those found guilty or regarded as guilty by association was established.

Right: The playwright Arthur Miller, who was called before the House Un-American Activities Committee, wrote The Crucible *(1953), set in Puritan New England, as an allegory of McCarthy's witch-hunt.*

So great was its influence that its victims found themselves out of work and shunned by their former colleagues.

In the Senate, McCarthy, together with his aides, the lawyer Roy Cohn (who was instrumental in securing the conviction of Julius and Ethel Rosenberg) and the anti-communist propagandist David Schine, intimidated, abused and terrified witnesses, as bogus allegations were made in an attempt to undermine the reputations of their enemies in public life. Nobody was immune from accusations that could destroy careers and ruin lives. In 1953, Robert Kennedy, who had worked for McCarthy as an assistant counsel, resigned because he "disagreed with the

Below: The 'Hollywood Ten' (included here) were screenwriters accused of being communists and were blacklisted by the industry.

way that the Committee was being run". In the same year, McCarthy mixed his personal and political agendas: when Schine was drafted, Cohn tried to influence the army into giving him special privileges. When the army refused, the senator supported Cohn, his chief counsel, and made the army a target for his investigations. It proved to be a fatal error.

In March 1954 Ed Murrow's exposé on his CBS programme, *See It Now,* concluded that "the line between investigating and persecuting is a very fine

one", and that McCarthy had "stepped over it repeatedly". From 22 April to 17 June, Americans could watch him in action. The Army–McCarthy hearings were broadcast to a nationwide audience on TV. As the hearings came to a close, Stuart Symington, the Democrat senator from Missouri, told McCarthy that his credibility had been destroyed: "The American people have had a look at you for six weeks. You are not fooling anyone." During almost 200 hours of broadcasting, the senator's methods had been held up to public scrutiny, and few liked what they saw. In December he was reprimanded by his peers for bringing the Senate into disrepute. The word 'censure' was excised from the final resolution. One of the senators who was absent from the vote was John F. Kennedy, who was then recovering from surgery on his back.

'McCarthyism' affected the lives of many Americans including a number of high-profile casualties, among them Charlie Chaplin, who in 1952 left the United States to travel to Europe. His right to re-enter the country was revoked. Meanwhile the prominent black actor and singer Paul Robeson was denied the right to leave the country when his passport was taken away. After the Senate reprimand, McCarthy went into terminal decline. Losing his battle with the bottle, he died from the effects of alcoholism in 1957.

ELVIS PRESLEY
AND THE NEW CULTURE OF YOUTH

In 1954, an unknown teenager walked into the studios of Sun Records in Memphis, Tennessee, and asked to make a recording. Known as the Hillbilly Cat, he sang locally with two backing guitarists and a drummer, who made up a band known as the Blue Moon Boys. A poor white boy from the South, who had grown up listening to black music – gospel and rhythm and blues – Elvis Presley was singing his way to fame. The following year, now managed by Colonel Tom Parker (the military title was strictly honorary) he signed with RCA Victor, who acquired his recording contract from Sun for an unprecedented $35,000. In 1956, 'Heartbreak Hotel' became his first chart-topping hit.

Presley represented one side of the 'generation gap' that was emerging in the 1950s – the decade that invented the 'teenager'. Increasingly, the musical taste of the new generation also defined their attitudes and lifestyle. Elvis combined black musical influences with

dance movements that some found suggestive and others thought provocative. He was 'Elvis the Pelvis'.

In June 1956, he sang his version of 'Hound Dog' on television, delighting the younger members of the studio audience but causing consternation among adults. His performance was condemned as vulgar and obscene in

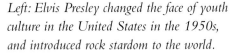

Left: Elvis Presley changed the face of youth culture in the United States in the 1950s, and introduced rock stardom to the world.

the press, but the ratings were huge. When he next sang the song on television, Elvis appeared in a tuxedo and addressed the song to a live basset hound. It led to three appearances on *The Ed Sullivan Show*, during which the camera focused on him solely from the waist up and he earned an endorsement from the host: "This is a real decent, fine boy. You're thoroughly all right."

Through records, live concerts, further television appearances and Hollywood movies, Elvis Presley rapidly became an icon of contemporary US popular culture. In 1958, he embarked on two years of military service, earning promotion to sergeant just prior to being discharged in March 1960. His recording company had issued a succession of hit singles and albums during his absence, and he resumed his recording and movie career.

In December 1970, 'the King' met the president. Presley had written to Richard Nixon, offering to become a federal agent-at-large in the Bureau of Narcotics and Dangerous Drugs. He had made "an in-depth study of drug abuse and communist brainwashing techniques" and was well placed to help deal with the problems posed by the counterculture. At the White House, he presented Nixon with a World War II vintage Colt .45. In return, the president gave him a federal badge of office. The photograph of their meeting is the single most requested item in the US National Archives.

Seven years later, addicted to prescription drugs, Elvis Presley died at Graceland, his home in Tennessee.

Left: Elvis and President Nixon in the Oval Office at the White House.

THE SPACE RACE
SPUTNIK, 1957

On 4 October 1957, Americans looking into the night sky could see Sputnik I, no bigger than a basketball, orbiting the Earth. For the next few weeks they might also hear the triumphant beep of its radio signal reminding them that the Soviet Union had beaten the United States into space. *Pravda*, the Russian newspaper, could not resist boasting: "Artificial earth satellites will pave the way to interplanetary travel, the new socialist society makes the most daring dreams of mankind a reality." The starting gun had been fired in the Space Race: the Cold War competition between the superpowers to explore the horizons beyond planet Earth was under way.

President Eisenhower belittled the Russian achievement. It was "one small

ball in the air". The following month, another Sputnik carried a dog into space. It was not until 31 January 1958 that the United States managed to launch its first satellite, Explorer I, only a fraction of the weight of its Soviet competitors. Later that year, Eisenhower approved the establishment of the National Aeronautics and Space Administration (NASA). Its task would be to put Americans into space.

On 12 April 1961, the cosmonaut Yuri Gagarin orbited the earth in *Vostok I*. He was the first man in space, and the Americans had been beaten again. President John F. Kennedy, who had exploited fears of a 'missile gap' opening between the United States and the Soviet Union in his campaign for the White House, responded with a bold commitment. On 25 May, just 20 days after Alan Shepard had made the USA's first successful sub-orbital flight, the new president appeared before

Left: The Russian cosmonaut Yuri Gagarin gave the Soviets a propaganda triumph when he became the first man in space.

Above: The USA was the first country to land a man successfully on the moon and return him to Earth. The mission was a defining moment in history.

Congress and announced an ambitious goal to be achieved within the decade: the United States would be first to put a man on the moon.

In February 1962, John Glenn in *Friendship 7* became the first American to make an orbital flight. The United States rapidly caught up and emphatically overtook the Soviet space programme. On 20 July 1969, five months before Kennedy's deadline expired, *Apollo 11* astronauts Neil Armstrong and Edwin 'Buzz' Aldrin stepped on to the moon's surface from the lunar landing vehicle *Eagle*, spending a total of two and a half hours there before rejoining Michael Collins in the command module *Columbia*.

President Nixon met the crew on their return to Earth. Americans no longer feared that, in Lyndon Johnson's words, they would have to sleep "by the light of a Communist moon".

THE CUBAN REVOLUTION

1959

Thomas Jefferson was 33 years old when he wrote the Declaration of Independence. Fidel Castro was the same age when, in 1959, after a three-year guerrilla campaign, he forced the Cuban dictator, Fulgencio Batista, into exile. With Castro were Raúl, his younger brother, as well as an Argentinean doctor, Ernesto 'Che' Guevara, and Cambio Cienfuegos, who came from a family of Spanish anarchists. Fidel became leader of the revolutionary government along with Raúl and Che. A few months after the revolution had succeeded, Cienfuegos, second only to Fidel in popularity among Cubans, disappeared on a flight to Havana. His plane was never found.

With Castro in power in Cuba, the United States had a problem close to home. Fidel Castro was no Thomas Jefferson. Soon after taking power, he legalized Cuba's communist party. On 28 February 1959, he suspended elections. The Eisenhower administration became convinced that if not yet a communist himself, Castro was taking Cuba towards communism. American

Below: Che Guevara became a global icon for revolutionaries.

Above: The Bay of Pigs invasion was a dramatic failure: Cuba remained a communist thorn in the USA's side.

sanctions prevented Cuba from exporting sugar, its main cash crop. Further trade restrictions followed. Anti-Castro Cubans who were able to leave the island headed for the nearest city on the American mainland: Miami.

On 26 September 1960, Castro addressed the United Nations General Assembly. To laughter and applause, he claimed that though the State Department demanded immediate compensation for the US assets seized on the island, Cuba could not afford to pay, and anyway, "We were not 100 per cent Communist yet. We were just becoming slightly pink."

The Americans were not amused. In 1954, the CIA had backed a coup in Guatemala that had overthrown its president, Jacobo Arbenz. The same fate was planned for Castro. When Cuba became an issue in the 1960 presidential election, Nixon, who knew of the administration's intentions, was forced to keep silent while Kennedy accused the Republicans of being 'soft' on Cuban communism. Three months after his inauguration, Kennedy authorized

the Bay of Pigs invasion. It was a complete failure. While sustaining heavy casualties, Cuban forces repelled the invasion and took over a thousand prisoners. Castro remained in power.

On 9 October 1967, in Bolivia, government troops operating under the direction of the CIA captured and killed Che Guevara. He became an iconic symbol of 1960s revolutionary fervour, not only in Cuba and Latin America, but across the world.

Below: Fidel Castro led Cuba for almost 50 years before stepping down in 2008.

JOHN F. KENNEDY
1961–1963

President for just over a thousand days, Kennedy's premature death made him a tragic hero whose potential to lead the United States during a troubled decade was unfulfilled. In the words of the title of a book by his close friends, *Johnny, We Hardly Knew Ye*.

John F. Kennedy was an outsider. He was born into a large Irish-American Catholic family in Massachusetts. His health was never robust but his family's wealth ensured a privileged upbringing. After graduating from Harvard in 1940, Kennedy joined the navy during World War II and commanded a motor torpedo boat – *PT 109* – in the South Pacific. It was sunk by a Japanese destroyer. Kennedy's actions in ensuring that he and his crew survived and were rescued became the stuff of heroic legend. His elder brother, Joe, was not so fortunate. He was killed flying a high-risk bombing mission in Europe, and John inherited his father Joseph's ambition for a son to become president.

Above: Kennedy's tragic death shaped the public's memory of his presidency and ensured his enduring popularity.

Born: 29 May 1917, Brookline, Massachusetts
Parents: Joseph (1888–1969) and Rose (1890–1995)
Family background: Business, public service
Education: Harvard College (1940)
Religion: Catholic
Occupation: Author, public service
Military service: Lieutenant, US navy, World War II
Political career: US House of Representatives, 1947–53
US Senate, 1953–61
Presidential annual salary: $100,000 + $50,000 expenses (refused by Kennedy)
Political party: Democrat
Died: 22 November 1963, Dallas, Texas

Elected to Congress in 1947, his political career progressed in the House of Representatives and then in the Senate. He married Jacqueline Bouvier in 1953. Kennedy's health problems – malaria, Addison's disease and chronic back pain – meant that he attended Congress infrequently. In 1956 he was recovering from life-threatening back surgery when he published the Pulitzer Prize-winning *Profiles in Courage*, an examination of key moments in the Senate's history. In the same year he tried unsuccessfully to become the Democrats' vice-presidential candidate.

His 1960 campaign for the presidency, managed by his brother Robert, was an insurgency, capturing the nomination through accumulating support in the primary elections. Kennedy's charismatic appeal helped defuse the issue of his religion: no Catholic had

JACQUELINE KENNEDY

The youngest first lady of the 20th century, Jacqueline Bouvier was 24 when she married John F. Kennedy in 1953. They had three children, only two of whom, Caroline and John, survived to adulthood. As first lady she added glamour and sophistication to the Kennedy White House, and supervised its restoration, appearing on television to give Americans a guided tour of her achievement. Five years after Kennedy's assassination, she shocked many Americans when she married Aristotle Onassis, the Greek shipping magnate, who was 23 years her senior. Widowed again in 1975, she lived the remainder of her life in New York, where she worked in publishing. She died in 1994.

Below: Jacqueline Kennedy was one of the youngest ever first ladies.

ever been elected to the White House in what remained a predominantly Protestant nation. His father's money helped his cause. He won the closest presidential election of the 20th century by just over 100,000 votes. He was 43 years old.

Above: The Kennedy family in 1934, with John F. Kennedy pictured third from right.

THE CHALLENGES OF OFFICE

In his speech accepting the Democrat nomination, Kennedy had talked of the United States being on the edge of a 'New Frontier' of "unfulfilled hopes and dreams". This campaign slogan summed up the feeling of optimism surrounding his administration as he took office. The challenges of political reality rapidly became apparent.

Kennedy inherited from Eisenhower the plan to invade Cuba. In April he took action, and the Bay of Pigs was a disaster. Two months later, the president met Khrushchev face to face for talks in Vienna, to try to defuse international tensions. Kennedy felt that the summit had not gone well: he had not convinced the Soviet leader of the USA's intent to stand firm against communist expansion. South-east Asia was a potential testing ground for US resolve. The president reportedly

Below: Kennedy's campaign for the White House was groundbreaking: he was the first Catholic to be elected president.

admitted: "Now we have the problem of making our power credible and Vietnam looks like the place." The former capital of what was now a divided Germany was another Cold War flashpoint. In August 1961, the Soviets built the Berlin Wall.

Lacking support in Congress, Kennedy did not achieve as much as he anticipated in terms of domestic legislation. He faced increasingly difficult confrontations, particularly in the South, where segregation was still rife, though under siege. The Civil Rights movement worked to overcome the 'Jim Crow' laws in education and transportation. The Kennedy administration, and notably Robert Kennedy as

THE 'NEW FRONTIER'

John F. Kennedy first used this phrase in his acceptance speech at the Democrat national convention in Los Angeles in 1960. The concept of the 'New Frontier' symbolized his determination to create a mood of activism, both at home and abroad, after what was widely felt to have been the complacency of the Eisenhower years. It was summarized in the most famous line of his inaugural address, when he invited his "fellow Americans" to "Ask not what your country can do for you – ask what you can do for your country."

attorney general, supported the protesters against intransigent Southern governors and violent racist reactions.

There were some lighter times. With the Kennedys as popular hosts, the White House became the social, cultural and intellectual centre of the New Frontier. In April 1962, at a dinner honouring 49 Nobel Prize-winners, Kennedy famously observed that it was

Below: The Cuban Missile Crisis could have ended in nuclear war: its peaceful resolution was Kennedy's greatest triumph.

MARILYN MONROE

"I can now retire from politics after having had 'Happy Birthday' sung to me in such a sweet, wholesome way." It was 19 May 1962. John Kennedy had almost turned 45 and the party was at Madison Square Garden, New York. The performer was Marilyn Monroe. Just under three months later, she was dead.

Born in 1926, Marilyn Monroe was the iconic blonde of the age: the perfect blend of glamour and Hollywood stardom in the post-war era of US celebrity. After a brief first marriage that ended as her career took off, in 1954 she married the legendary baseball player, Joe Di Maggio. A year later they divorced.

Her relationship with the playwright Arthur Miller lasted longer: their marriage endured for five years, ending in 1961. During that time Arthur Miller wrote the screenplay for *The Misfits*, the last film she would complete. During filming she had a nervous breakdown.

By the time she sang at Madison Square Garden, she knew both Jack and Bobby Kennedy well, having been introduced to them by their brother-in-law, Peter Lawford. She allegedly had affairs with both of them.

Her premature death at 36 from barbiturate poisoning, officially recorded as "probable suicide", unleashed a torrent of speculation in which the mystery surrounding her last hours, together with the potent mix of celebrity, sex and politics, led conspiracy theorists to argue that it was the Kennedys who were responsible for her murder. She remains an American icon, preserved in the memory of generations of fans and of those who knew her.

It was Joe Di Maggio who continued to leave flowers at Marilyn's grave.

Above: Marilyn Monroe's death and her relationship with the Kennedys remains the subject of popular debate.

probably the greatest concentration of genius that had been present in the White House, with the possible exception of when "Thomas Jefferson dined alone".

The defining moments of Kennedy's presidency came during 13 days in October 1962. He negotiated his way through the Cuban Missile Crisis, triggered by the discovery that the Soviets were placing missiles in Cuba and bringing the world to the brink of nuclear war. His reputation soared in the United States and overseas. In June 1963, he travelled to Berlin. Standing in front of the Wall, he proclaimed his support for the city: "*Ich bin ein Berliner*" ("I am a citizen of Berlin").

Throughout his presidency, the situation in South-east Asia had been volatile. Kennedy sent US military advisors to South Vietnam while the regime of its leader, Ngo Dinh Diem, crumbled in the face of increasing internal opposition to his authoritarian rule. On 1 November 1963, Diem died in a coup.

Three weeks later, Kennedy travelled to Dallas, Texas. On 22 November, as his motorcade left the airport for the city, he told Jacqueline, who was accompanying him on the visit, that they were heading into "nut country". As the presidential limousine slowly travelled along Elm Street, Nellie, wife of the Texas governor John Connally, said to him,

"You can't say Dallas doesn't love you, Mr President". Moments later he was assassinated. After a state funeral in Washington DC, John F. Kennedy was buried in Arlington National Cemetery.

Below: John F. Kennedy and Nikita Khrushchev met for the first time at the Vienna summit, in 1961.

THE BERLIN WALL
1961

Berlin was a divided city. The Allied occupation after World War II established the US, British and French zones in its western part, and the Soviet sector in the east. An isolated outpost, West Berlin became the scene of tense confrontation and dramatic events as the Cold War played out in Europe. In June 1948, it was blockaded. Only daily supplies delivered by Allied planes until September 1949 prevented it from being starved into submission.

In 1952, following the establishment of the Federal Republic of Germany in the west and the German Democratic Republic in the east, the border between the two states was closed. Berlin remained a chink in the 'Iron Curtain': until 1957, when it was forbidden, it was still possible to travel from the eastern to the western zones, either with permission or, at greater risk, without it. Many East Germans took advantage of this to trade a life under communism for one in West Germany.

Below: A worker builds the Berlin Wall.

Above: The Brandenburg Gate, which was designed as a symbol of peace. It became a symbol of German power.

By the time Kennedy and Khrushchev met in Vienna in 1961, the Soviet leader wanted control of the city. Kennedy stood firm and the war of words threatened to end in military action. The crisis was defused. The president recognized the Soviet leader's problem, telling Walt Rostow, one of his security advisors: "East Germany is haemorrhaging to death … He has to do something to stop this. Perhaps a wall." By signalling his concern to protect West Berlin rather than the entire city, Kennedy gave Khrushchev an exit strategy. On 13 August 1961 the first rudimentary structure was built. The following day, the Brandenburg Gate in the city was closed, but the route from West Berlin to the Federal Republic stayed open. It signalled a compromise. As Kennedy put it: "A wall is a hell of a lot better than a war."

Kennedy was not the only US president to visit Berlin. In 1987, Ronald Reagan stood in front of the Brandenburg Gate and famously invited his Soviet counterpart, Mikhail Gorbachev, to "Tear down this Wall." On 9 November 1989, it came down, symbolizing the end of the Cold War and paving the way for Germany's reunification the following year.

Below: The Wall came down in 1989 as communist regimes throughout Eastern Europe lost power or were overthrown.

THE CUBAN MISSILE CRISIS
1962

The Soviet Union had placed missiles in Cuba that were capable, as Khrushchev later recalled, of devastating "New York, Chicago, and the other huge industrial cities, not to mention a little village like Washington". President Kennedy now faced the most serious confrontation of the Cold War. During the crisis, he walked the tightrope across the abyss of nuclear war, and after 13 days of intense debate, public action and secret diplomacy, he made it safely to the other side.

On 14 October 1962 a United States U-2 surveillance flight over Cuba confirmed the presence of missile bases there. Although there was no evidence that nuclear warheads were also on the island, with Soviet ships on the way, the United States feared that it was only a matter of time before they arrived. Kennedy brought together a group of advisors from the National Security Council, dubbed 'ExCom', to determine what should be done.

One option was a high-risk pre-emptive strike to destroy the missiles on Cuba, but Kennedy was concerned that such a move would provoke Soviet retaliation and a reciprocal attack on Berlin. The president's brother Robert Kennedy, who emerged as a key member of ExCom, together with Robert McNamara, the secretary of defense, argued in favour of the more prudent course of action that was eventually taken: the setting up of a naval blockade to prevent the Soviets from delivering more missiles or warheads to Cuba.

After it had been given a less aggressive title, the president announced the "quarantine" in a nationwide television address on Monday 22 October. Two days later it went into effect. On Wednesday 24 October, Russian ships approached the quarantine zone, which was patrolled by US forces. They stopped,

Above: The Cuban Missile Crisis saw the world teeter on the brink of escalation to nuclear war.

then turned away. The secretary of state, Dean Rusk, famously observed: "We're eyeball to eyeball and I think the other fellow just blinked."

With the missiles still in place, Kennedy's military advisors pressed for an invasion of the island. On Friday 26 October, the president received a letter from Khrushchev, proposing that if the United States pledged not to take military action in Cuba, then the missiles would be dismantled and removed. The following day, the Soviet leader, under pressure from his own military, sent another, less conciliatory message: it demanded that as part of any

Left: Castro's militiamen train for conflict in the mountains of Cuba.

resolution to the crisis the United States should remove the nuclear weapons it had stationed in Turkey.

ROBERT KENNEDY

It was Robert Kennedy who found a way out of the confusion caused by the contradictory statements made by the Soviet leader: they should ignore the second letter and proceed on the basis of what had first been suggested. He had good reason to believe that this tactic would work. Throughout the crisis, he had been meeting secretly with the Soviet ambassador, Anatoly Dobrynin. He had already hinted that the president might find a missile trade acceptable. Late at night on Saturday 27 October, after his brother had made a public pledge not to invade Cuba, Robert Kennedy met once more with Dobrynin and gave him private assurances that the United States would remove its nuclear capability from Turkey. There was also an ultimatum: the Soviet Union must agree to this secret compromise within 24 hours, or the United States would take military action against Cuba. Earlier that day, a U-2 plane photographing sites for an

invasion had been shot down over the island and its pilot had been killed.

Khrushchev ended the crisis. The following morning, on Radio Moscow, it was announced to a somewhat bewildered Russian audience, who had not known about the existence of the missiles on Cuba, that they would be dismantled and taken away. By April the following year, the USA's missiles in Turkey were quietly scrapped.

As a result of the missile crisis, the 'hot line' was set up allowing rapid and direct communication between leaders in Washington and Moscow. Cold War rhetoric softened. As Kennedy put it in a speech on 10 June 1963: "In the final analysis, our most basic common link is that we all inhabit this small planet. We all breathe the same air. We all cherish our children's future. And we are all mortal."

Below: Reconnaisance flights by the US military showed a Russian attack submarine close to Cuba.

Above: While war seemed imminent, a resolution to the crisis was negotiated away from the public gaze.

THE HOT LINE

During the tense negotiations of the Cuban Missile Crisis, it had taken nearly 12 hours to receive and decode a 3,000-word letter from Khrushchev, showing the value of a reliable, fast and easy method of communication between the presidents of the United States and the Soviet Union. The hot line, or 'red telephone' between the White House and the Kremlin was set up by an agreement signed in Geneva on 20 June 1963. It was first used during the Six Day War between Egypt and Israel in 1967, during which the superpowers kept each other informed of naval movements in the area that might otherwise have appeared provocative.

THE ASSASSINATION OF KENNEDY
1963

At lunchtime in Dallas on Friday 22 November 1963, John F. Kennedy was on his way to the city's Trade Mart to deliver a speech in which he planned to talk about peace. He was travelling in a presidential motorcade, in an open-top car so that everyone could see him. Among the spectators was Emile Zapruder, who had with him his home movie camera. He would capture the moment that an assassin's bullet would once again claim the life of a United States president.

He was an easy target. As the motorcade passed the Texas School Book Depository building, President John F. Kennedy was shot and fatally wounded. More than 40 years later, there is much about his assassination that remains controversial. The story of his presidency is sometimes over-whelmed by the desire to speculate on the drama of his death.

Kennedy was rushed to Parkland Hospital, but he had already succumbed to his traumatic injuries: no recovery was possible from the bullet that had hit him in the head. On television, the CBS newscaster, Walter Cronkite, made the announcement: "From Dallas, Texas, the flash, apparently official. President Kennedy died at 1 p.m. Central Standard Time, two o'clock Eastern Standard Time." Cronkite, 'the most trusted man in America', removed his glasses and appeared to shed a tear.

MURDER OF THE MURDERER

Within 90 minutes of the assassination, Lee Harvey Oswald, a former marine who had spent time in the Soviet Union, was apprehended on suspicion of the murder of J. D. Tippit, a Dallas police officer, who had tried to arrest him. Oswald worked at the Book Depository, had been witnessed leaving the building shortly after the shooting and was the owner of the mail-order rifle found at the scene. He was charged with the president's assassination. Two days later, while being transferred to the county jail, in front of a watching tele-vision audience, Lee Oswald was shot dead by Jack Ruby, a Dallas strip-club owner. Initially found guilty and sentenced to death, Ruby's conviction was subsequently overturned. He died in 1967 while awaiting a new trial for Oswald's murder.

The Warren Commission, set up by President Lyndon Johnson, sat for ten months and concluded that Oswald had acted alone. It was one of several gov-ernment investigations, all of which have returned the same verdict. None has done anything to undermine

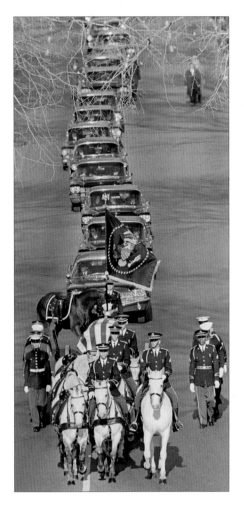

Above: Kennedy's state funeral was attended by dignitaries from more than 90 countries.

popular belief that the assassination was a conspiracy, and it is still the subject of widespread speculation.

On 17 March 1964, St Patrick's Day, in his first major speech after his brother's death, Robert Kennedy quoted from a poem written for the Irish hero Owen Roe O'Neill:

> *We're sheep without a shepherd,*
> *When the snow shuts out the sky –*
> *Oh! Why did you leave us, Owen?*
> *Why did you die?*

Left: The moment the bullet hit Kennedy in his open-top cavalcade as it travelled past the Book Depository.

CHAPTER FOUR

LYNDON B. JOHNSON TO JIMMY CARTER

1963–1981

BETWEEN 1963 AND 1981 THE PRESIDENCY
EXPERIENCED POLITICAL TURBULENCE
UNPARALLELED IN ITS 20TH-CENTURY HISTORY.
PUBLIC CONFIDENCE IN THE INSTITUTION
COLLAPSED. THOSE WHO HELD THE OFFICE HAD
THEIR CREDIBILITY, PERSONAL INTEGRITY AND
CAPACITY TO PROVIDE NATIONAL LEADERSHIP
DOUBTED, QUESTIONED AND FOUND WANTING.
IN THE LIGHT OF THE ASSASSINATION OF JOHN F.
KENNEDY, WHOSE STATURE WAS IMMEDIATELY
ASSURED, OTHER PRESIDENTS FAILED TO MEASURE
UP. ONE WAS A CASUALTY OF WAR, ANOTHER AN
HEROIC FAILURE; THEIR TWO SUCCESSORS PROVED
UNABLE TO RESTORE THE PRESIDENCY TO ITS
FORMER POSITION AS THE LYNCHPIN OF THE
US POLITICAL SYSTEM. LYNDON B. JOHNSON,
RICHARD NIXON, GERALD FORD AND
JIMMY CARTER ALL LEFT OFFICE WITH A
SENSE OF PROMISE UNFULFILLED.

*Left: The hostage crisis in Tehran finally ended on the day that
Jimmy Carter left office.*

LYNDON B. JOHNSON
1963–1969

Lyndon Johnson's presidency was a political watershed: he was the first candidate from a former Confederate state to be elected. His support of civil rights ushered in the end of the Democrats' domination of Southern politics, which had endured since reconstruction, and re-established the region as a place from which presidents might be elected.

Johnson was born in Texas in 1908, into a family whose roots went deep into the history of the Lone Star State. He left high school at the age of 15 and drifted to California, before returning to enrol at Southwest Texas State Teachers College in 1927. After graduating he taught briefly before going to Washington in 1931 as secretary to Congressman Richard Kleberg. He was elected to the House of Representatives in 1936, but failed

Above: Johnson was never able to escape from the shadow that memories of John F. Kennedy cast over his presidency.

in his first attempt to become a senator four years later. He served briefly in the navy during World War II. In 1948 he finally reached the Senate amid charges of ballot-rigging in a disputed election. Seven years later, Johnson was its youngest ever majority leader.

He recovered from a heart attack to become the most effective political operator the Senate had ever seen, relentlessly gathering information to help to win over fellow senators.

Kennedy thwarted his presidential ambitions in 1960, but Johnson accepted his rival's invitation to become his running mate. Marginalized as vice president in Kennedy's administration, he moved to centre stage on 22 November 1963, as president of a nation traumatized by the shock of the events in Dallas.

A DIFFICULT TASK

Johnson negotiated his first difficult days in the White House with sensitivity and skill. Though he came from the South, he championed civil rights, responding to the movement led by Martin Luther King Jr. Knowing the value of the

Below: Johnson takes the oath of office on Air Force One – the presidential plane – at Love Field in Dallas, Texas, witnessed by his predecessor's widow, still wearing the coat spattered with her husband's blood.

Born: 27 August 1908, near Johnson City, Texas
Parents: Samuel (1877–1937) and Rebecca (1881–1988)
Family background: Farming, public service
Education: Southwest Texas State Teachers College (1930)
Religion: Disciples of Christ
Occupation: Teacher, public service
Military service: Commander, US naval reserve, World War II
Political career: Congressional secretary, 1931–7
US House of Representatives, 1937–49
US Senate, 1949–61
Vice president, 1961–3
Presidential annual salary: $100,000 + $50,000 expenses
Political party: Democrat
Died: 22 January 1973, near Johnson City, Texas

political capital invested in the reputation of his assassinated predecessor, he exploited it, cajoling Congress to pass landmark legislation advancing the cause of racial equality as a tribute to Kennedy's memory. The legislation paved the way for women to press their case for equal rights as well. In January 1964, he announced his intention to declare "war on poverty" and in May he outlined his vision of the "Great Society" based upon "abundance and liberty for all" and demanding "an end to poverty and racial injustice". The Civil Rights Act, which he signed in July, was the most radical since reconstruction, and its architect was a president who came from a former Confederate state. The 'Great Society'

'LADY BIRD' JOHNSON

Above: Claudia Johnson's childhood nurse gave her charge the pet name 'Lady Bird'.

Claudia Taylor was born in Texas in 1912. Less than three months after graduating from the University of Texas she met Lyndon Johnson. They married in 1934 and had two daughters, Lynda Bird and Luci Baines. As first lady, she was a staunch advocate of civil rights and also campaigned for the conservation and enhancement of America's natural environment. She died on 11 July 2007, at the age of 94.

Above: In 1968 President Johnson signed the Civil Rights Act, also known as the Fair Housing Act, which prohibited discrimination in the sale, financing and rental of housing on the basis of race, religion and national origin. It has been updated twice to disallow discrimination on the basis of sex or disability.

Below: A contemporary cartoon depicts Johnson as a Texan cowboy, more at home with domestic than foreign policy.

was built in a flurry of legislation unmatched since Franklin Roosevelt's 'New Deal'. In 1965, Congress enacted its twin centrepieces, Medicare and Medicaid, extending health insurance provision for the elderly and those on low incomes.

FAILING FOREIGN POLICY

Johnson's substantial domestic achievements contrasted with his disastrous military intervention abroad. At the same time as radical domestic changes were being implemented, the question of involvement in Vietnam began to consume Johnson's attention.

The political situation in Vietnam had deteriorated quickly in the aftermath of Diem's assassination. "I knew from the start that I was bound to be crucified either way I moved," he said in an interview in 1970. "If I left the woman I really loved – the Great Society – in order to get involved in that bitch of a war on the other side of the world, then I would lose everything at home. But if I left that war and let the Communists take over South Vietnam, then I would be seen as a coward and my nation

Above: Johnson's presidency was characterized by widespread civil unrest. Race issues continued. Martin Luther King was assassinated and the war in Vietnam escalated intensifying the anti-war protests.

would be seen as an appeaser and we would both find it impossible to accomplish anything for anybody anywhere on the entire globe."

Johnson took a decision, and it proved to be a disastrous mistake. In August 1964, in response to alleged North Vietnamese attacks on US naval vessels, he asked Congress to approve the 'Tonkin Gulf' Resolution, authorizing the president to use military force there should it prove necessary. It was a 'blank cheque for war'.

Johnson did not cash his cheque immediately. During the campaign leading up to the presidential election in September that year he had pledged not "to send American boys nine or ten thousand miles away from home to do what Asian boys ought to be doing for themselves". Portraying his Republican opponent, Senator Barry Goldwater, as dangerously right wing in a world in

which China had just acquired nuclear weapons and Khrushchev had been ousted in the Kremlin had won Johnson a convincing victory.

As more and more troops were drafted to fight in Vietnam, opposition to the war escalated. At last, on 31 March 1968, increasingly beleaguered, Johnson effectively resigned from the presidency, announcing that he would not seek his party's nomination for a further term in office.

Johnson's presidency was further undermined by the enduring power of the myth of John F. Kennedy. His assassination had robbed the United States of a leader whose stature was assured the moment he was shot, and whose reputation was steadily embellished by a nation whose memories and perceptions were shaped by the events that had followed his death. If Kennedy had lived, would the United States have had to suffer the trauma of Vietnam?

As the nation's involvement in the conflict in South-east Asia grew, those who protested against Lyndon Johnson's war looked to Robert Kennedy to end it. He emerged from a period of introspection after his brother's death to

begin a political journey that led him to speak for the USA's dispossessed and to condemn the Vietnam War. But minutes after he had given his victory speech on winning the California primary, an assassin's bullet once more left the promise unfulfilled.

Johnson retired to his Texas ranch. He left office with his 'Great Society' rioting in the streets, protesting against the war he had made it fight. As a consequence, Lyndon Johnson's ambition to be regarded as the greatest president since Franklin Roosevelt was crushed by the USA's war in Vietnam. In 1973, his successor, Richard Nixon, told him privately that negotiations with the Vietnamese had been concluded in Paris. On 23 January 1974, Nixon announced that "peace with honor" had been achieved. But Lyndon Johnson had died the previous day.

TONKIN GULF

In August 1964, North Vietnamese torpedo boats were reported to have attacked US naval vessels off its coast in the Gulf of Tonkin. President Johnson ordered retaliatory air strikes and asked Congress to approve a resolution giving him the power to take further military action. Only later was it revealed that the incidents had been fabricated. In 1965, Johnson admitted: "For all I know, our Navy was shooting at whales out there." By then he had his pretext for war.

Below: The Tonkin Gulf resolution gave Johnson the authority to fight the Vietnam War.

ROBERT KENNEDY
ATTORNEY GENERAL AND NEW YORK SENATOR

Mount Kennedy, overlooking the Lowell Glacier in Canada close to the border with Alaska, was the highest unclimbed mountain in North America. In 1965 it was named in memory of Robert Kennedy's brother and in the same year, although he suffered from a fear of heights, Robert Kennedy made the first ascent of it. For him, courage was, as Ernest Hemingway defined it, 'grace under pressure'.

Robert Kennedy was born on 20 November 1925. He grew up in the shadow of his elder brothers, Joe and John, physically smaller but no less competitive. He was the seventh of nine children and, as he later recalled, "when you come from that far down you have to struggle to survive".

After graduating from Harvard in 1950, he married Edith Skakel. They had 11 children. He managed John F. Kennedy's 1952 Senate campaign and

Below: Robert Kennedy survived the initial shooting, but died later in hospital. Five others were also wounded.

the following year joined the staff of McCarthy's investigative committee. He did not stay long. Later he worked for the Senate committee investigating corruption in organized labour, gaining a national reputation for relentlessly pursuing the Teamsters' Union leader, Jimmy Hoffa. As his brother's campaign manager in the 1960 election, suspicion

Above: Sirhan Sirhan (beneath the raised arm) is held tight after his fatal attack upon Robert Kennedy.

that he opposed offering Lyndon Johnson the vice-presidential nomination led to their mutual hatred. When, after the assassination in Dallas, Johnson needed to know the exact wording of the oath of office, he telephoned the attorney general: Robert Kennedy. It was, as Lady Bird Johnson remembered, "an excruciating call".

ASSASSINATION

In 1964, Kennedy resigned as attorney general and was elected as a New York senator. Four years later, he ran for the presidency. He had been his brother's most trusted advisor, involved in key decisions, not least during the Cuban missile crisis. More radical, championing the dispossessed and aware of the limitations on the exercise of military power overseas, he had just won the California primary and seemed on course to secure his party's nomination when, on 6 June 1968, he was shot dead at the Ambassador Hotel in Los Angeles. He was 42 years old.

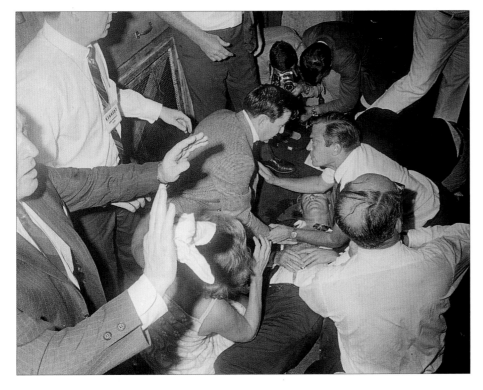

THE CIVIL RIGHTS MOVEMENT

The Civil Rights movement defined the domestic politics of the decade. It did not begin in the 1960s, but the accumulated grievances of a century's neglect meant that its pent-up political energy exploded during the Kennedy and Johnson administrations, as its supporters took their protest to the streets.

There was progress. The courts, the Congress and the president were forced to respond to the demand for racial equality. The campaign of civil disobedience aimed to achieve peaceful integration. For some it was not enough. A more radical movement, advocating 'black power', sought change through violent confrontations. Race remained a major fault line in US culture and society.

In Montgomery, Alabama, on 1 December 1955, Rosa Parks, a member of the NAACP, refused to give up her

Below: Civil rights protesters demonstrated to force the South to obey the Supreme Court ruling that segregation was unconstitutional.

seat on a bus to a white man, in defiance of the state's segregation laws. She was fined. In protest, blacks began a boycott of the city's public transportation system: their demonstration lasted for almost 13 months, until a Supreme Court decision forced an end to discrimination on the buses.

It was during the Montgomery bus boycott that a local Baptist minister emerged as an activist and civil rights leader: Martin Luther King Jr. In 1957, he became president of the Southern Christian Leadership Conference, which organized acts of non-violent civil disobedience, dramatizing the racial injustices that pervaded the South.

In 1960, four black students in Greensboro, North Carolina, staged a sit-in to draw attention to discrimination at a Woolworth's lunch counter. Similar protests took place elsewhere. Young blacks joined the Student Nonviolent Co-ordinating Committee (SNCC). Together with the Congress of Racial Equality (CORE) it organized a series of 'freedom rides': during the

BLACK PANTHER PARTY

The Black Panther party was founded in Oakland, California, in October 1966 to promote civil rights for African-Americans. Its militant and sometimes violent pursuit of black liberation led J. Edgar Hoover to describe it in 1969 as "the greatest threat to the internal security of the country". Its leaders were arrested and jailed. The party rejected the integrationist policy of Martin Luther King in favour of black nationalism. It espoused a radical socialist ideology and successfully organized welfare programmes among the poorest black communities.

spring and summer of that year groups of blacks and whites travelled together on buses throughout the South to see if laws banning segregation in interstate travel facilities were being observed. Their non-violent protests were met with violence as they were attacked by mobs of Southern whites.

CHANGING ATTITUDES

In October 1962, amid riots and with his safety in the hands of federal troops sent by President Kennedy, James Meredith became the first black student to enrol at the University of Mississippi. The following year, after Martin Luther King had been arrested and jailed in Birmingham, Alabama, more civil rights protests took place. Television audiences were able to watch the city's police chief, Eugene 'Bull' Connor, using dogs and fire hoses against those involved in the demonstrations. The Civil Rights movement gained support and momentum as a result. In August 1963, 200,000 people joined the 'March on Washington' and saw King give the speech that defined his image in the public's imagination.

Above: 'Freedom riders' travelling the South on interstate buses were met with hostility, not least from local police.

Black churches were bombed. Civil rights workers were murdered. The Ku Klux Klan gained fresh recruits in Southern states. Other black leaders, who were more militant than King, also gathered support. One was Malcolm X, then a spokesman for the Nation of Islam, who observed that, "The only people in this country who are asked to be non-violent are black people." He advocated black resistance to white intimidation and demanded more than the recognition of civil rights: "An integrated cup of coffee isn't sufficient pay for 400 years of slave labour." He maintained that the development of a distinctive black identity was necessary, based on a recognition of the reality of history: "We're not Americans, we're Africans who happen to be in America. We were kidnapped and brought here against our will from Africa. We didn't land on Plymouth Rock, that rock landed on us."

Malcolm X was assassinated in February 1965. The following year, Stokely Carmichael, leader of the SNCC, echoed his message and coined the expression 'Black Power', urging blacks "to unite, to recognize their heritage, and to build a sense of community action". Later he joined Bobby Seale and Huey Newton in the Black Panther party.

In 1968, Martin Luther King was assassinated and an increasingly fragmented Civil Rights movement seemed to lose some of its earlier momentum. But by then it had changed the landscape of American politics. The 'Jim Crow' laws constituting a system of legal apartheid in the South had been dismantled, and the racial hatred and moral hypocrisy of those who supported that system had been exposed. Attitudes would change only slowly but the movement had laid the foundations for the advance to a more racially tolerant US society.

Below: Rosa Parks' refusal to give up her seat to a white man sparked the Montgomery bus boycott.

MARTIN LUTHER KING JR
CIVIL RIGHTS ACTIVIST

On 3 April 1968 Martin Luther King Jr recalled the time a decade earlier, during a book signing in Harlem, when he had been stabbed by "a demented black woman". The *New York Times* reported that had he sneezed it would have been fatal. He was, he said, "so happy that I didn't sneeze". The following evening he was assassinated at a motel in Memphis. He was 39 years old.

Martin Luther King had been an ordained minister for 20 years. In 1954, he became pastor at the Dexter Avenue Baptist Church in Montgomery, Alabama. During the city-wide bus boycott, he was elected president of the Montgomery Improvement Association, which co-ordinated the protest, going on to help form the Southern Christian Leadership Conference to press for civil rights reform. He visited India in 1959, returning "more convinced than ever before" that Gandhi's philosophy of "non-violent resistance is the most potent weapon available to oppressed people in their struggle for justice and human dignity".

In 1960 King was arrested and jailed in Atlanta after a sit-in at a restaurant. John F. Kennedy, campaigning for the presidency, phoned Coretta King in support of her husband's action. His brother Robert called Georgia's governor and King was freed.

Imprisoned again in April 1963, he wrote the 'Letter from a Birmingham Jail' in which he defended his actions against the charge that they were 'unwise and untimely'. The time was now. Three months later, King gave his most famous address to the crowds in front of the Lincoln Memorial after the 'March on Washington', sharing his

Above: King, leader of the Civil Rights movement, advocated peaceful protest.

dream that racial equality would be achieved. The following year he was awarded the Nobel Peace Prize.

In 1965, in Selma, Alabama, King led a campaign to register black voters and was arrested once more, along with many of his supporters. It dramatized the struggle for civil rights, as King was able to point out in a national newspaper advertisement that "there are more Negroes in jail with me than there are on the voting rolls." Towards the end of his life he became more radical. In 1967 he criticized the USA's involvement in Vietnam as "one of history's most cruel and senseless wars". His violent death sparked riots in cities across the United States.

In 1986, the third Monday in January was designated as a federal holiday, Martin Luther King Day. Only two other individuals have been honoured in this way: Christopher Columbus and George Washington.

Left: Thousands of people marched on Washington to hear King deliver his "I have a dream…" speech in 1963.

WOMEN'S RIGHTS

Just as women had taken up the cause of abolitionism in the 19th century, seeing affinities between their repressed position in society and the plight of black slaves in the South, so in the 20th century their demand for gender equality became part of the broader struggle for civil rights.

In 1961, President Kennedy appointed Eleanor Roosevelt to chair his Commission on the Status of Women. In order to highlight the contemporary problems of discrimination against women in the workplace, the commission would have needed to look no further than NASA. Although a number of women were selected as potential astronauts in the initial Mercury space programme, none of them had the opportunity to emulate the achievement of Valentina Tereshkova, who in 1963 became the Soviet Union's first female cosmonaut.

That same year, the writer and activist Betty Friedan published *The Feminine Mystique*. In it, she questioned the traditional stereotypes of women as mothers and homemakers: "We can no longer ignore that voice within women that says: 'I want something more than my husband and my children and my home.'" Three years later, Friedan was a founder member of the National Organization for Women (NOW), which aimed "to take action to bring women into full participation in the mainstream of American society now, exercising all the privileges and responsibilities thereof in truly equal partnership with men". It rapidly became the most powerful feminist lobbying group in the United States.

In 1973 the Supreme Court decided the case of Roe v. Wade, brought by a pregnant woman against the State of Texas. She contested the constitutionality of the Texas law restricting the legality of abortion to cases in which it

was medically prescribed in order to save the mother's life. The Court declared state anti-abortion laws unconstitutional, igniting a political firestorm that still rages in contemporary American political life. The 'right to choose' and the 'right to life' define alternative perspectives on what still remains, both for women and for men, a complex and difficult decision.

The women's movement failed to achieve its goal of adding an equal rights amendment to the Constitution, but more women were encouraged to participate in politics, running successfully for elective office at both state and national levels. Presidents responded to

Above: National Organization for Women president Betty Friedan and other feminists march in New York City on 26 August 1970, on the 50th anniversary of the passing of the Nineteenth Amendment, which granted American women full suffrage. The organization called upon women nationwide to strike for equality on that day.

the demand for gender equality by appointing women to the Supreme Court and to Cabinet offices including those of attorney general and secretary of state but throughout the 20th century some 'glass ceilings' remained firmly intact, not least that of the Oval Office itself.

THE VIETNAM WAR

CIRCA 1959–1975

In 1961, after his Vienna summit meeting with Khrushchev, President Kennedy met with President de Gaulle, who predicted that if Americans were to become involved in a war in Vietnam, "you will, step by step, be sucked into a bottomless military and political quagmire". He spoke from experience. In 1954 the French defeat at Dien Bien Phu had abruptly ended the French attempt to re-impose colonial control in South-east Asia.

Vietnam was divided, with Ho Chi Minh's nationalist government in the North and the US-backed regime of Ngo Dinh Diem in the South. Many Vietnamese regarded this settlement as temporary and awaited a reunification election. The problem was that Ho Chi Minh, who looked likely to win it, was a communist. The United States refused to hold the election; instead, Americans imagined an independent democratic nation called South Vietnam. They tried to build it and were then forced to defend it. It was the biggest foreign policy debacle of the 'American Century'.

By the time Kennedy came to the White House, Diem's regime in South Vietnam was in serious trouble. The North Vietnamese Army (NVA) together with the guerrilla insurgents of the Viet Cong (VC) were fighting the army of the Republic of Vietnam (ARVN) in a civil war that became a war of national liberation. For the United States, it was always a military rather than a foreign policy problem: to oversee the administration's policy on

Above: As the Vietnam War escalated, more and more Americans were drafted to fight in a strange and unfamiliar land.

Vietnam, Kennedy chose Robert McNamara, his secretary of defense, rather than Dean Rusk, the secretary of state. Even before its troops were committed in numbers, it had become the USA's war as well.

In 1962, McNamara was confident. On a visit to South Vietnam he argued that "every quantitative measure …

KHE SANH AND TET

The siege of the isolated US base at Khe Sanh, near the North Vietnamese border, took place between January and March 1968. It became part of the Tet offensive – named for the Vietnamese New Year celebrations in which it started. Khe Sanh and Tet symbolized the tenacity of the Vietnamese in resisting the USA's military intervention.

VIETNAMIZATION

President Nixon's policy of Vietnamization was aimed at shifting the burden of fighting the Vietnam War from the US forces to the South Vietnamese army. The United States still provided the military hardware, but the policy, which was the basis of the 'Nixon Doctrine', allowed the progressive withdrawal of American troops from South-east Asia.

Above: The Vietnam Veterans Memorial in Washington DC is one of the most visited memorials in the nation's capital city.

Above: Despite the USA's overwhelming fire power, Vietnamese resistance broke its resolve.

shows that we are winning the war". The following year, in his State of the Union address, Kennedy claimed: "The spearpoint of aggression has been blunted in South Vietnam." Soon afterwards, the political situation spiralled out of control, culminating in a coup against Diem by officers of the South Vietnamese Army and his assassination. Three weeks later, Lyndon Johnson inherited the presidency with an avowed intention: "I am not going to lose Vietnam. I am not going to be the president who saw South-east Asia go the way China went."

McNamara later realized the reality: "We had no sooner begun to carry out the plan to increase dramatically US forces in Vietnam than it became clear that there was reason to question the strategy on which the plan was based." US technology, firepower and military resources were overwhelmingly superior to those of the North Vietnamese and Viet Cong. The United States controlled the battlefield in a war of attrition. What could not be won was the struggle for the 'hearts and minds' of the Vietnamese. When a US army officer admitted that "it was necessary to destroy the village in order to save it", the futility of the US enterprise became clear.

In 1967, the administration claimed that there was "light at the end of the tunnel". The following year, the 'credibility gap' was confirmed. The Siege of Khe Sanh was swiftly accompanied by the Tet offensive. Americans watched on television as their embassy in Saigon was besieged by enemy troops. Fierce fighting developed around the old imperial capital of Hue. The psychological impact in the United States during a presidential election year was profound. Walter Cronkite, reporting the news from Vietnam, saw no sign of victory: "To say that we are mired in a stalemate seems the only realistic, yet unsatisfactory, conclusion." On 31 March Johnson announced a bombing pause as a prelude to peace negotiations

Below: Helicopters were used extensively to move troops quickly during the Vietnam War.

and said that he would not seek another term in the White House.

Richard Nixon came to the presidency with a 'secret plan' to end the war. It involved one last effort to win it, expanding the conflict into the neighbouring countries of Laos and Cambodia. 'Vietnamization' allowed US forces to be withdrawn. In 1973, the president's claim of 'Peace with Honor' allowed Americans to avoid recognizing the painful reality of defeat. Two years later, the last US helicopters clattered away from Saigon as the North invaded the South and Vietnam was reunified. As the Vietnam veteran and poet W. D. Ehrhart observed: "Didn't we think we bestrode the world. Didn't we have a lot to learn."

THE COUNTERCULTURE

The 'credibility gap' between what the president said and what the people believed, which emerged during Lyndon Johnson's time in the White House, symbolized an increasingly divided society. The political energies of the 1960s produced radical change and a younger generation prepared to question authority. They discovered personal empowerment in ways that ran counter to the accepted political, economic and social structures of the Cold War United States. The counterculture thrived on public displays of opposition to what it identified as the conformist values constraining society. The contrast between the 1950s and the 1960s can be seen in the actions of two icons of their times. Whereas in 1958, Elvis Presley obeyed his summons to serve in the US military, eight years later Muhammad Ali refused to be drafted to fight in Vietnam.

The counterculture's questioning of US values, and its perceived threat to traditional morality, produced its own reaction. Evangelical religion sought a

Below: The Kent State University shootings during a protest against the Vietnam War punctured the idealism of the counterculture.

transformation of US society, placing its interpretation of faith at the centre of what became an influential political organization.

On 9 May 1970, before dawn, President Richard Nixon surprised a group of anti-war demonstrators gathered at the Lincoln Memorial. The meeting was reported in *Time* magazine: "Before he left, Nixon said: 'Just keep it peaceful. Have a good time in Washington, and don't go away bitter.' " He was speaking across a political and cultural divide. Opposing the war had become a principled commitment among those whose values the president did not share and could scarcely understand.

They were members of the counterculture. Belonging meant being young and adopting a lifestyle that revolved around sex, drugs and rock 'n' roll. Nixon's early morning encounter in Washington happened ten years to the day after the Food and Drug Administration had approved the contraceptive pill for marketing, ushering in the 'sexual revolution'.

EMERGING YOUTH CULTURE

San Francisco led the way. By the mid-1960s, youth culture had emerged and hippies were spreading a gospel of 'free love'. In 1967, thousands converged on the Haight-Ashbury district for the 'Summer of Love'. The previous year, Timothy Leary had popularized the use of LSD with the catchphrase: "Tune in, turn on and drop out." The soundtrack was the music played at iconic events such as the Woodstock Festival in August 1969.

The Vietnam War was the catalyst for political activism, and 'flower power' was the slogan of non-violence adopted by those who burned their draft cards and refused to serve overseas. Protest became street theatre. In October 1967, during

WOODSTOCK

For three days in August 1969, around 400,000 people gathered at a farm in New York State for the Woodstock Music & Art Fair. Members of the rock 'n' roll aristocracy, including Janis Joplin, The Who, The Grateful Dead, Canned Heat, Crosby, Stills, Nash and Young, Jimi Hendrix, Joan Baez and Ravi Shankar played at an event that, for the counterculture, encapsulated the spirit of the times.

Above: Woodstock remains a symbol of the liberalism of the age.

a demonstration in Washington, Abbie Hoffman and Jerry Rubin, leaders of the Youth International Party – 'Yippies' – announced that they would levitate the Pentagon to exorcise the 'evil spirits' within the building.

On 4 May 1970, students at Kent State University in Ohio placed flowers in the rifle barrels of National Guard troops during an anti-war demonstration on campus. Four were shot dead and nine were wounded. It was a symbolic moment: a shock of reality after a decade of idealistic dreams. Looking back, Abbie Hoffman would admit: "The 60s are gone, dope will never be as cheap, sex never as free, and the rock and roll never as great."

MUHAMMAD ALI

President Kennedy took an interest in boxing. In 1962, he invited Floyd Patterson to the White House. Patterson was a role model for the National Association for the Advancement of Colored People and was about to defend his world heavyweight title against Sonny Liston, an ex-streetfighter with a conviction for armed robbery. Kennedy told the champion he had to win for the sake of the Civil Rights movement. Patterson lost.

Two years later, Liston was beaten in turn by Cassius Clay, who would win the world heavyweight title twice more over the next 15 years, justifying his nickname, 'The Greatest'. A gold medallist at the 1960 Olympics in Rome, Clay was distinguished by his exceptional speed and style, and between 1960 and 1963 he was undefeated in 19 fights. Born in 1942 in Louisville, Kentucky, he was the son of a billboard painter and had been raised as a Baptist. But in 1964 at the time of the title fight with Liston he joined the Nation

of Islam, renouncing his name (like Malcolm X, he rejected the names given to his slave ancestors) and becoming Muhammad Ali.

In 1965, Floyd Patterson fought him for the heavyweight title. Ali, he said, had "taken the championship and given it to the black Muslims". Beating him "would be my contribution to civil rights". Patterson lost again.

Patterson later confessed: "I came to love Ali. I came to see that I was a fighter and he was history." Ali's reputation rests not just on his unparalleled boxing ability, but also on his actions outside the ring. In 1967, he refused to be drafted to serve in Vietnam. He was stripped of his title, fined and sentenced to a five-year prison term; while free, pending his appeal, he was barred from the boxing ring. He could not fight, but he could still talk. Support for his stand against the draft grew as public opinion turned increasingly against the war, and Ali became a popular speaker on university campuses across the country.

Above: Muhammad Ali and Malcolm X in 1964.

In 1970, he regained his boxing licence. After winning two comeback fights, in 1971 he went into the ring with Joe Frazier. Once more cultural symbolism surrounded a title fight, pitting Frazier as the unwilling representative of the establishment against the insurgent Ali. Frazier won a unanimous points decision. It was Ali's first professional defeat. His reaction was simple: "I whupped him." Later that year, he won his own unanimous decision, when the Supreme Court overturned his conviction for draft evasion.

Ali regained his title, knocking out George Foreman, in 1974. It was as much a political statement as it was a sporting achievement. He had dramatized the struggle against the Vietnam War and for black civil rights. "Man, I ain't got no quarrel with them Viet Cong," he said. "No Viet Cong ever called me nigger."

Left: Muhammad Ali became heavyweight champion by beating Sonny Liston. In the re-match in 1965, many at the ringside did not see his controversial 'phantom punch' which ended the fight.

SOCIAL UNREST
1968

"The spirit of resistance to government is so valuable on certain occasions, that I wish it to be always kept alive. It will often be exercised when wrong, but better so than not to be exercised at all. I like a little rebellion now and then. It is like a storm in the atmosphere." Thomas Jefferson had expressed this opinion in 1787. In 1968, protesters all over the world took him at his word. Sometimes the spirit was successful in bringing about change. On other occasions resistance was crushed.

In a decade of transformations, 1968 was a pivotal year. In January, Jeanette Rankin, who in 1916 had been the first woman to be elected to Congress and who had voted against the resolution supporting the USA's entry into World War I, led a march on Capitol Hill to demonstrate against the Vietnam War. With Rankin, then aged 87, were 5,000 women, including Coretta Scott King, the wife of Martin Luther King, and the folk singer and activist Judy Collins.

On 16 March US troops took part in the massacre of hundreds of South Vietnamese civilians at My Lai. In the United States the depth of anti-war sentiment was revealed in the same month when in the Democrat primary in New Hampshire, Eugene McCarthy, the 'peace candidate', did much better than expected.

In Europe, French universities closed amid a wave of strikes, as protest against the government peaked during the May 'events'. Students took to the streets and engaged in battles with the police, and the strikes spread until about ten million workers were involved. There was no revolution, as some had feared, but the protests brought down the Gaullist government and inspired similar student action all over Europe and in South America.

The 'Prague Spring', a liberalization of the communist regime orchestrated

by Alexander Dubček, ended in August when Warsaw Pact troops and tanks invaded Czechoslovakia. In the Middle East, a coup in Iraq brought the Baath party to power. One of its leaders was Saddam Hussein. The arab leader Yasser Arafat took control of the Palestine Liberation Organization.

During October, students led violent demonstrations in Mexico City. At the Olympic Games there, which had been boycotted by most African nations in protest at South Africa's apartheid regime, successful black US athletes gave

Left: American sprinters Tommie Smith and John Carlos raise their fists and give the black power salute at the 1968 Olympic Games in Mexico City. The move was a symbolic protest against racism in the United States. Smith, the gold medal winner, and Carlos, the bronze medal winner, were subsequently suspended from their team for their actions.

the black power salute while receiving their medals.

As television images recorded the tumult of events, 1968 became memorable as a year that symbolized a decade of dramatic political, social and cultural change across the United States and the world. In particular Americans witnessed not only death and destruction abroad, caused by their continued involvement in the Vietnam War, but also the assassinations of Martin Luther King Jr and Robert Kennedy at home.

There were riots on the streets of Chicago during the Democrats' national convention, which nominated Hubert Humphrey, Lyndon Johnson's vice president, as the party's candidate. In November the Republican party's candidate, Richard Nixon, defied political expectations after his defeat in 1960, and won the presidential election by a narrow margin. He would be the creative architect of a new foreign policy, heralding a shift in the USA's relations with China and the Soviet Union. As the year drew to a close, on 24 December, as Apollo 8 orbited the moon, in a live television broadcast, its crew read passages from the book of Genesis.

Left: The national guard were deployed during two days of rioting, arson and sniping that took place on the streets of Chicago during the Democrats' national convention in 1968. Police vehicles were covered in barbed wire.

RICHARD NIXON

1969–1974

He was a loner, an ardent American football fan and a successful poker player; he was an actor caught out in a lie. He changed the way the United States thought about the world, becoming the first president to visit communist China and building a new relationship with the Soviet Union based upon détente – reducing the international tension that had characterized the Cold War world.

Born in California in 1913 and brought up a Quaker, Nixon won a scholarship to Harvard, but his family could not afford the additional expense of an education so far from home. Instead, he attended the local Whittier College, where he played football with more enthusiasm than skill and continued to do well academically. He won a scholarship to Duke University law school in North Carolina.

Nixon spent World War II as a government lawyer in Washington and then in the navy in the Pacific, where he became the popular proprietor of a beer and hamburger stand, 'Nick's Snack Shack'. In 1946 he won election to the House of Representatives as a Republican with what became his trademark campaign style: the suggestion that his opponent had communist sympathies. He rapidly gained national attention by successfully revealing Alger Hiss as a former communist. In 1950,

Below: Spiro Agnew was Nixon's running mate in 1968 and 1972. In 1973 he resigned after a tax evasion scandal.

Above: Nixon set new directions for US foreign policy until the Watergate scandal destroyed his presidency.

Nixon was elected to the Senate and two years later, not yet 40, he became vice president elect.

During Eisenhower's administration, Nixon's high-profile anti-communist reputation was enhanced when he faced hostile demonstrations in Latin America and argued the merits of capitalism with Khrushchev in their impromptu 'kitchen debate' in an American showhouse at an exhibition in Moscow. After losing the 1960 presidential election, he stood for election as governor of California. He lost again. Even he appeared to believe his career was over, but he was bluffing. In 1968, a 'new Nixon' re-entered the political arena as president of the United States.

A NEW VISION

Nixon's interest was in foreign policy. With Henry Kissinger as his national security advisor, Nixon began to implement a vision that belied his earlier intransigent anti-communist

attitudes. His reputation as a hardline Cold Warrior gave him the political capital to spend on his innovative overtures to China and the Soviet Union without fear of being accused of being 'soft on communism'.

He was helped by the recognition of the cracks that had appeared in the apparent monolith of international communism. Nixon arrived in the White House two years after the Cultural Revolution in China, and while the Soviet Union was reinforcing its military on the border between the two nations.

In 1971, Henry Kissinger secretly visited China, paving the way for Nixon's historic meeting with Mao Zedong, chairman of the Communist party of China, in Beijing in February the following year. That May Nixon travelled to Moscow for a summit

---

Born: 9 January 1913, Yorba Linda, California
Parents: Frank (1878–1956) and Hannah (1885–1967)
Family background: Farming, store-keeping
Education: Whittier College (1934), Duke University Law School (1937)
Religion: Quaker
Occupation: Lawyer, public official
Military service: Commander, US naval reserve, World War II
Political career: Attorney, US Office of Emergency Management, 1942
US House of Representatives, 1947–51
US Senate, 1951–3
Vice president, 1953–61
Presidential annual salary: $200,000 + $50,000 expenses
Political party: Republican
Died: 22 April 1994, New York, New York

Above: Nixon with his secretary of state William Rogers (left) and Soviet leader Leonid Brezhnev (right) at the signing ceremony for the SALT treaty.

meeting with Leonid Brezhnev and to sign the treaty resulting from two and a half years of strategic arms limitation talks (SALT). In November, Nixon won re-election in a landslide.

In 1969 Nixon introduced a lottery: those, including a young Bill Clinton, whose birthdays were assigned high numbers in the draw, no longer faced the draft. Fewer troops were in Vietnam. Nevertheless opposition to the war continued. Peace negotiations dragged on in Paris.

In 1969, Nixon had authorized the covert invasion of Cambodia as part of his 'Vietnamization' policy, targeting Viet Cong bases and underlining US support for the South Vietnamese government. The *Pentagon Papers*, published in June 1971, revealed classified information about the history of United States intervention in South-east Asia and how the policies leading to the unwinnable war there had been made. It caused

political polarization, and domestic anti-war protests increased. Soon afterwards the White House recruited 'plumbers', so-called because they were to be responsible for stemming the flow of unauthorized leaks to the media.

During the 1972 election campaign, Nixon returned to his political roots, sanctioning a clandestine campaign of 'dirty tricks', in which members of the infamous Committee to Re-Elect the President (CREEP) solicited illegal

campaign contributions and identified their opponents as enemies who should be targeted with electronic surveillance. On 17 June 1972 burglars were arrested at the Democrat National Committee's offices in the Watergate building in Washington. They were there to plant bugging devices, but the significance of their actions lay not so much in the attempt itself as in the administration's actions immediately after the break-in. It was eventually revealed that a cover-up of the White House's involvement in the events at the Watergate building was orchestrated by Nixon's top advisors and the president himself. 'Watergate' became a shorthand expression for the corrupt practices that Nixon condoned in his pursuit of power.

Nixon's second term was overwhelmed by the scandal of Watergate. On 8 August 1974 he resigned rather than face impeachment. He spent the remainder of his life attempting to restore his political reputation by writing a series of books that drew on his experiences as an international statesman. He died in 1994. President Bill Clinton was among those who delivered eulogies at his funeral.

Left: Henry Kissinger being sworn in as secretary of state in September 1973. He was the first foreign-born citizen of the United States to become the nation's top diplomat.

WATERGATE

1974

The Watergate break-in was more than a burglary. The president had assumed he was above the law. It was one thing to exploit loopholes in the fabric of United States constitutionalism. It was another to abuse the Constitution itself.

When Richard Nixon ordered a cover-up of his administration's involvement in breaking and entering at the Watergate building, it was because he had other things to hide. Investigative reporters eventually lifted the curtain on a web of political corruption that had corroded his presidency, and Congress assumed its role in checking and balancing the executive. Public trust evaporated: the president was forced to resign. The aftershocks of Watergate continue to shape the limits of presidential power. Nixon's successors in the White House have had to beware of popular suspicions that they may be assuming more power than is granted to them by the Constitution.

"One of the five men arrested early Saturday in the attempt to bug the Democratic National Committee head-quarters is the salaried security co-ordinator for President Nixon's re-election committee." The lead paragraph in a story in the *Washington Post* on Monday 19 June 1972, two days after the break-in, appeared under the by-lines of Bob Woodward and Carl Bernstein. Once the link between the burglars and the White House had been established, the media had their story. It was Woodward and Bernstein who pursued it with remarkable tenacity.

They followed the trail of illegal campaign contributions and uncovered the plans for political espionage and sabotage that were part of the effort to guarantee that Nixon's bid for re-election would be successful. Guided by sources within the administration, Woodward and Bernstein were able to name those senior members of the Nixon administration involved in the scandal. Those sources included the infamous 'Deep Throat', named after a notorious pornographic movie of the time, who in 2005 was revealed as Mark Felt, then deputy director of the FBI.

In September 1972, Woodward and Bernstein wrote a story alleging that John Mitchell, who had resigned as director of the Committee to Re-Elect the President (CREEP) in the month following the break-in, had controlled a secret fund that had financed illegal political activities – including the electronic surveillance of the president's opponents in public life and the media – while he had been serving as Nixon's attorney general. Mitchell denied the charge. He was later sent to jail. By April 1973, two of the president's closest aides, John Ehrlichman and Bob Haldeman, had also been implicated in the scandal and were forced to resign, along with Mitchell's successor as attorney general, Richard Kleindienst. John Dean, the president's legal advisor, was fired. As Nixon put it, "there can be no white-wash at the White House".

Below: When the extent of his complicity in the Watergate scandal was revealed, Nixon resigned rather than face impeachment.

Above: Senator Sam Ervin (centre) whose congressional investigation into Watergate revealed that Nixon had bugged himself.

Dean appeared before the Senate Watergate Committee and in its televised hearings testified that he had met frequently with the president to discuss the Watergate cover-up. Senator Howard Baker asked what became a famous question: "What did the president know and when did he know it?" The answers came tantalizingly close when, in July 1973, Alexander Butterfield, a former White House aide, revealed that the president, who was accused of bugging others, had also bugged himself, routinely taping conversations and telephone calls in the White House.

There were more political casualties as Nixon fought to prevent the tapes being made public. When transcripts were released, they revealed a president who habitually used profanities – 'expletive deleted' became a refrain – and fulminated against those he thought were conspiring against him.

In November, he was still protesting his innocence. "People have got to know whether their President is a crook. Well, I'm not a crook." Few believed him. Congressional pressure

increased. In July 1974, the House of Representatives approved the first of three articles of impeachment that charged the president with the obstruction of justice.

AN AUTHORIZED COVER-UP

On 5 August, the 'Smoking Gun', the incriminating evidence that confirmed the president's complicity in the attempt to subvert the course of justice in the aftermath of the Watergate burglary, was found. Taped conversations were released revealing that Nixon had authorized the cover-up and ordered

the FBI not to proceed with its investigation of the break-in. Three days later, the president announced his resignation. He left office the following day.

Three years later, Nixon tried to justify his behaviour and explain his actions. In one of a series of televised interviews with David Frost, broadcast in May 1977, he argued that "When the president does it that means it is not illegal." With 45 million Americans among a worldwide audience, Nixon appealed to the precedent set by Abraham Lincoln during the Civil War. In a time of national emergency, Lincoln had claimed that, "Actions which otherwise would be unconstitutional, could become lawful if undertaken for the purpose of preserving the Constitution and the Nation."

The Vietnam War, like the Civil War, had divided the United States. During wartime, Nixon declared, "A president does have certain extraordinary powers which would make acts that would otherwise be unlawful, lawful." He was wrong. Richard Nixon's concern was self-preservation, rather than protecting the national interest.

Below: Carl Bernstein (left) and Bob Woodward (right) were the investigative journalists who pursued the cover-up all the way to the Oval Office.

GERALD FORD
1974–1977

Gerald Ford did not give an inaugural address. In his remarks on taking the oath of office he talked of "the lonely burdens of the White House". He could "only guess at those burdens" although he had "witnessed at first hand the tragedies that befell three presidents and the lesser trials of others".

Ford was a member of the Warren Commission, which had investigated Kennedy's assassination. He had been minority leader in the House of Representatives during Johnson's presidency and had become Nixon's unelected deputy as vice president. Now he was the USA's first unelected president. He inherited a White House that was suffering the effects of the aftershocks from the political upheavals of the previous decade. His transparent honesty was a refreshing change from his predecessor's secretiveness. Ford

Above: After 25 years in Congress, Gerald Ford was appointed vice president, inheriting the White House when Nixon resigned.

worked hard to restore public faith in the presidency, but it was difficult.

He was named for both his father and his stepfather. He was born Leslie King in 1913, but two years later his parents divorced. In 1916, his mother re-married and her son was brought up in Grand Rapids, Michigan, as Gerald Ford Jr. He won a sports scholarship to Michigan State University, then went to law school at Yale. He graduated in 1941. After war service in the navy, he returned to Grand Rapids where he practised law. In 1948, the year of his marriage to Betty Bloomer Warren, he was elected to Congress, and gradually rose through the ranks of the Republican party.

POLITICAL CAREER

While the Democrats remained the majority party in the House of Representatives, Ford became leader of the Republican minority in 1965. In 1973, after Spiro Agnew (Nixon's vice president) had been forced to resign amid charges of corruption, Ford, who had remained as minority leader in the House, succeeded him as vice president. Eight months later, Nixon resigned.

TWO YEARS IN OFFICE

Ford had been in office a month when he pardoned Nixon, believing it was necessary to move the country on and avoid the prospect of a former president facing criminal charges in court. His popularity plummeted. In 1975 Cambodia seized the *Mayaguez*, a US merchant ship that it claimed had strayed into its territorial waters. Ford authorized military action and the vessel was recaptured. The action gave a boost to national confidence in the aftermath of the Vietnam War.

Despite his efforts to restore public trust in the presidency, Ford could not escape the shadow of Watergate. In 1976, he lost his bid to be elected in his own right. His memoirs were called *A Time to Heal*. That challenge remained. Ford died in 2006 at the age of 93.

BETTY FORD

Born Elizabeth Bloomer in Chicago in 1918, she married William Warren at 24, divorced in 1947, and married Gerald Ford the following year. They had four children. She was candid about her addictions to painkillers and alcohol, and open about her surgery and treatment for breast cancer, raising public awareness of these issues.

Below: In 1982 Betty Ford established the Betty Ford Center for the treatment of drug and alcohol dependency in California.

Born: 14 July 1913, Omaha, Nebraska

Parents: Leslie (King) (1881–1941) and Dorothy (1892–1967)

Stepfather: Gerald (Ford) (1890–1962)

Family background: Business (sales)

Education: University of Michigan (1935), Yale University Law School (1941)

Religion: Episcopalian

Occupation: Lawyer, public official

Military service: Lieutenant commander, US naval reserve, World War II

Political career: US House of Representatives, 1949–73

Vice president, 1973–4

Presidential annual salary: $200,000 + $50,000 expenses

Political party: Republican

Died: 26 December 2006, Rancho Mirage, California

RELIGION AND POLITICS

The success of the Civil Rights movement, the failure of Vietnam and the revelations of the Watergate scandal meant that presidents now surveyed a new and often unfamiliar landscape of United States politics. Religion became more important in shaping political allegiances. The ideological consensus among liberals that the Cold War had to be fought aggressively to contain the threat of communist expansion fragmented. Some liberals, appalled by the outcome of the Vietnam War, opposed further military intervention overseas. Others, who became known as neo-conservatives, argued that the United States should still be able to project its military power overseas in support of its foreign policy ambition to remain the world's dominant superpower. Meanwhile, the 'Imperial Presidency' went into retreat. The USA's bicentennial celebrations in 1976 were edged with apprehension about its future.

During the 1960s the black churches of the American South had led the call for civil rights. In the following decade, white evangelists, particularly in the South, reacting against what they saw as the erosion of moral standards, entered the political arena. In 1979, Jerry Falwell co-founded the 'Moral Majority': it was

Above: Bicentennial celebrations took place throughout America in 1976, and helped bring closure to an era of discontent.

pro-life, anti-gay, in favour of strengthening US defence, against liberalism. Fundamentalist Christians found a political home within the Republican party and have since remained a force in national politics.

Senator 'Scoop' Jackson from Washington State supported Lyndon Johnson's policy on Vietnam. A staunch anti-communist, he tried for the Democrats' presidential nomination in 1972 and 1976, but his views were increasingly at odds with the outlook of his party. Two of his aides, Richard Perle and Paul Wolfowitz, like other Democrats who became concerned that the 'Vietnam Syndrome' was acting as a constraint on the president's power, joined the Republicans and became leading neo-conservative advocates of a more forceful foreign policy.

THE IMPORTANCE OF FAITH

In 1976, evangelical religion helped Jimmy Carter become the first former state governor since Franklin Roosevelt to become president. Carter was a Democrat whose Baptist faith was rooted in Christian tolerance. He disappointed many with fundamentalist convictions, who found political

sanctuary within the Republican party. The Imperial Presidency, the product of the ideological consensus established at the beginning of the Cold War, had crashed and burned in the political firestorms of Vietnam and Watergate. Presidents now faced the challenge of leading a more disunited USA as the nation's conflicting views on issues of moral concern, fuelled by a resurgence of religious activism, continued to rage.

THE IMPERIAL PRESIDENCY

Arguing that Johnson during Vietnam and Nixon during Watergate had ignored the principles of American constitutionalism, the historian Arthur Schlesinger Jr coined the term 'Imperial Presidency' to describe their abuses of executive power. As Congress reasserted its authority, it seemed that the presidency was more 'imperilled' than 'imperial' and the proper limits of presidential power have remained under constant debate.

THE VIETNAM SYNDROME

The public's reluctance to support US military intervention overseas after the debacle of Vietnam was seen initially by liberals as a useful restraint on the president's power. The so-called 'Vietnam Syndrome' later came to be viewed by neo-conservatives as an obstacle to be overcome, so that the use of military power could once more be an option should the USA's commander-in-chief deem it necessary to send troops to war.

JIMMY CARTER
1977–1981

Jimmy Carter, a born-again Christian from the former confederate South, campaigned better than he governed and once in power rapidly lost his electoral appeal. While Carter realized what was wrong with the United States, he could do little to put it right.

Carter was born in rural Georgia, growing up in a house that did not have electricity or indoor plumbing. His parents owned a peanut farm. In 1943 he entered the US Naval Academy in Annapolis, and three years later he married his sister's best friend, Rosalynn Smith. For the next seven years, he worked on the development of the USA's nuclear submarines, retiring from the navy in 1953 and returning to manage the family farm.

In 1958, Carter refused to join the White Citizens Council, which had been established to resist desegregation. As a result his business was temporarily boycotted. Four years later he embarked on a political career. In 1962 he won a seat in the State Senate after successfully contesting the electoral fraud that had occurred during the Democrat primary contest. In 1966 he was tempted to enter federal politics by running for Congress. Instead he chose to campaign to become governor of Georgia. He was comprehensively beaten in the

Above: Little went right in Jimmy Carter's presidency, but he became a respected elder statesman of US politics.

primary election. Out of politics, and after a period of introspection, he became a 'born-again' Christian. Thereafter, religion became central to his life and public service. He stayed out of the political arena while the Vietnam War tore the Democrats apart, returning in 1970 to be elected as Georgia's governor. From his vantage point in Atlanta he watched Nixon entangle himself in the web of Watergate. When he ran for president in 1976, 'Jimmy Who?' was an outsider, distanced from the divisions of Vietnam and untainted by the corruption of the political establishment in Washington. He won a narrow victory.

DOMESTIC POLICY

Carter's first action was to declare a 'blanket pardon' for Vietnam draft resisters. The wording was important: an amnesty would have implied forgetting; a pardon symbolized forgiveness. Carter then confronted the realities of governing. He was unable to establish a

constructive relationship with Congress. The 'outsiders' who accompanied him to Washington, along with the president himself, were treated first with suspicion and then with outright hostility.

Carter's programme to conserve energy was the outcome of a growing realization that the USA's profligate consumption of natural resources was not only environmentally unsustainable but also made its economy vulnerable to fluctuations in the price of oil. He described his campaign to reduce energy consumption as one which would "test the character of the American people and the ability of the President and the Congress to govern". His policy did reduce US dependency on foreign oil but was complex and difficult to understand. As the economy worsened, the public simply saw longer lines at gas stations and paid higher prices for fuel.

CAMP DAVID

Carter attempted to shift US foreign policy towards a concern with human rights. In 1978, he brokered the Camp

Born: 1 October 1924, Plains, Georgia

Parents: James (1894–1953) and Lillian (1898–1983)

Family background: Peanut farming

Education: US Naval Academy, Annapolis (1946)

Religion: Baptist

Occupation: Farmer, public official

Military service: Lieutenant, US navy

Political career: Georgia State Senate, 1963–6

Governor of Georgia, 1971–5

Presidential annual salary: $200,000 + $50,000 expenses

Political party: Democrat

Below: Fuel shortages in the United States, caused partly by the Iranian revolution, resulted in panic buying.

Above: Carter allowed the deposed Shah into the United States, unleashing a storm of anti-US protests in Iran.

David accords between Menachem Begin and Anwar Sadat, which led to the negotiation of a peace treaty between Israel and Egypt the following year. It was the high point of his presidency. By the following year, he was increasingly unpopular with the public at home. In July he gave what came to be known as his 'malaise' speech, although he never used that word to describe "a crisis that strikes at the very heart and soul and spirit of our national

will". He identified its cause: "We were taught that our armies were always invincible and our causes always just, only to suffer the agony of Vietnam. We respected the Presidency as a place of honor until the shock of Watergate. These wounds are still very deep. They have never been healed." He could not supply the cure.

The Middle East, the backdrop for his greatest success, now damaged his presidency beyond repair. In November 1979, Islamic militants in Iran occupied

Below: Jimmy Carter, Anwar Sadat and Menachem Begin at Camp David.

the American embassy in Tehran, taking 52 hostages who were only released on the day Carter left office. It would not be the last time that political turmoil in the Middle East had an impact upon the reputation of a US president.

Carter's post-presidential career has been as illustrious as his presidency was disappointing. The Carter Center in Atlanta has advanced his human rights agenda. In his work for Christian aid organizations such as 'Habitat for Humanity', his involvement in monitoring worldwide democratic elections, his writings, and as recipient of the Nobel Peace Prize in 2002, Jimmy Carter has taken to heart the admonition of his favourite poet, Dylan Thomas: "Do not go gentle into that good night."

ROSALYNN CARTER

Born Rosalynn Smith in Plains, Georgia, in 1927, she married Jimmy Carter at the age of 18. They had four children. A politically active first lady, she attended Cabinet meetings and National Security Council briefings. She chaired the Presidential Commission on Mental Health, and remains fully involved with the activities of the Carter Center in Atlanta.

THE IRANIAN HOSTAGE CRISIS

1979–1981

In 1953, President Eisenhower approved a CIA plan to stage a coup against Mohammad Mosaddeq, Iran's prime minister, whom the agency suspected had communist sympathies. Power was to be consolidated in the hands of the king, Reza Shah Pahlavi. US military equipment and Iranian oil money would support the Shah's regime. The coup was successful but the United States was now dependent on the Shah to keep Iran as an oil-rich pro-Western power in the Middle East.

In 1963, the Shah managed to quell growing religious protest against secularization and political unrest at the uneven distribution of wealth in the country. Iran's spiritual leader, the Ayatollah Khomeini, whose supporters had led the protests, was exiled. He eventually settled in France where he remained a focus of opposition to the Shah. Throughout his years in exile, he continued to influence Iranians who worked to undermine the Shah's hold on power. It was 16 years before they were successful.

In 1979, the United States was a bystander as a new round of protests escalated into a full-scale Islamic revolution, which forced the Shah to flee the country. Khomeini returned to Tehran as the popular leader of the revolution and the main influence shaping the future of Iranian politics. The revolutionaries abolished the monarchy and an Islamic Republic was established in its place.

Should the Shah of Iran, now travelling from country to country in exile and suffering from terminal cancer, come to the United States? Jimmy Carter asked his advisors. Later, his vice president, Walter Mondale, recalled that most of them favoured letting the Shah into the country. Carter then asked what action they would recommend should the Iranians react by taking the

staff in the USA's Tehran embassy hostage. In Mondale's words: "No one had an answer to that. Turns out, we never did." In October 1979 the Shah was allowed to come to the United States to receive medical treatment.

STORMING THE EMBASSY

The following month the Tehran embassy was occupied by Islamic militants who held 52 diplomats hostage, and the crisis dominated the remaining 14 months of Carter's presidency. His first response was to use economic

Below: US hostages being paraded by their militant captors on the first day of the crisis that ended Carter's presidency.

Above: Demonstrators storm the United States embassy in Tehran and set fire to the US flag.

sanctions and diplomacy to secure the hostages' release. Under domestic pressure for more dramatic action, on 11 April 1980 he tried a high-risk military rescue operation, but a desert sandstorm disrupted the mission and a helicopter crashed, causing eight US service personnel to lose their lives. The rescue attempt ended in failure and public humiliation for the United States and its president.

The crisis became a symbol of both the president's weakness and the USA's loss of international prestige in the post-Vietnam era. Carter persevered with frustrating negotiations that dragged on while his re-election campaign foundered: the lengthy crisis effectively ejected him from the White House.

The hostages were finally released minutes after his successor had taken the oath of office. It was as a private citizen and representative of President Reagan that Jimmy Carter flew to an emotional meeting with the released hostages in Germany on 21 January 1981.

CHAPTER FIVE

RONALD REAGAN TO THE PRESENT DAY

1981–

ATTEMPTED ASSASSINATION, POLITICAL SCANDAL, MILITARY INTERVENTION IN THE MIDDLE EAST, IMPEACHMENT, A DISPUTED ELECTION AND THE 'WAR ON TERROR': AS THE 20TH CENTURY ENDED AND THE 21ST CENTURY BEGAN, THE US PRESIDENT CONTINUED TO BE AT THE EPICENTRE OF THE NATION'S POLITICAL LIFE. THREE FORMER STATE GOVERNORS, ONE FORMER VICE PRESIDENT AND ONE FORMER SENATOR WON THE EIGHT ELECTIONS HELD BETWEEN 1980 AND 2008. THREE WERE REPUBLICANS AND TWO WERE DEMOCRATS. ONE WAS THE OLDEST EVER TO OCCUPY THE WHITE HOUSE AND TWO WERE AMONG THE YOUNGEST TO BECOME CHIEF EXECUTIVE. THE OTHER TWO WERE FATHER AND SON. GEORGE W. BUSH'S LEGACY, THE CONTINUING WARS IN AFGHANISTAN AND IRAQ, REMAINED A CHALLENGING INHERITANCE FOR THE 44TH PRESIDENT OF THE UNITED STATES.

Left: Every president since Reagan has authorized the use of the USA's military power, most controversially George W. Bush in his prosecution of the "war on terror".

RONALD REAGAN

1981–1989

Ronald Reagan was the first president since Eisenhower to complete two full terms in office. He was a politician who had once been a Hollywood star. He auditioned for the role of president, won election to the White House, and then turned in a performance that, if not flawless, was a tough act to follow. The oldest elected president defied conventional political stereotypes. Reagan's life spanned the 'American Century' and proved to him the limitless potential of the 'American Dream'.

He was born in Illinois in 1911. His family was of modest means, its resources further stretched when his father battled alcoholism. Ronald Reagan graduated from Eureka College in 1932, the same year that he first voted in a presidential election – as a Democrat supporting Roosevelt.

After working as a radio sports announcer in Iowa, in 1937 he was offered a contract in Hollywood by

Below: After the assassination attempt which almost killed Reagan, his press secretary James Brady (in the light blue suit) lies severely wounded.

Above: Ronald Reagan, 'The Great Communicator', left office as popular as when he entered it: a rare achievement.

Warner Brothers. In 1940, he married Jane Wyman. They had a daughter and adopted a son before divorcing nine years later. Reagan's film career, notable for an early role as football coach George Gipp in *Knute Rockne – All American* (1940) continued through the war years, during which he made

training films for the armed services. He won critical acclaim for his performance in *Kings Row* (1942). In 1947, he became president of the Screen Actors Guild and was active in its campaign against communism in Hollywood. He married Nancy Davis in 1952. As Reagan's movie career stalled, he found a new audience as the host of the Sunday evening television show *General Electric Theater*, touring the country as a speaker for its sponsor.

In 1962, he became a registered Republican. Four years later he was elected to the first of two terms as governor of California. After two unsuccessful bids for the Republican presidential nomination in 1968 and 1976, in 1980 he became its candidate, winning the White House in a landslide. A little under three weeks before his 70th birthday celebrations, he was inaugurated as the USA's 40th president.

A NEW ERA

Reagan did much to restore national self-confidence with his breezy optimism and infectious enthusiasm for the American Dream. His ability as the 'Great Communicator' was reminiscent of Franklin Roosevelt. At his best he was a visionary. At his worst, his lack of attention to the illicit activities of his subordinates ensnared him in the Iran–Contra scandal. It could have led to his impeachment. That it did not had much to do with Reagan's personality: even his opponents were charmed by his relaxed good humour.

Reagan was lucky to survive more than ten weeks: like James Garfield, he was the victim of an assassination attempt in Washington DC on 30 March 1981. Medical science had improved in the intervening century, and his life was saved. His remarks as he faced emergency surgery confirmed his strength of character. To Nancy it was:

Above: Over 3,000 people attended the rally in 1986 outside the American embassy in London to register 'disgust' at the United States' bombing of Libya. Reagan tried to reassert America's military power after the Vietnam War.

"Honey, I forgot to duck." To his surgeons it was: "I hope you're all Republicans." Within a month he had recovered sufficiently to seek support

Born: 6 February 1911, Tampico, Illinois
Parents: John (1883–1941) and Nelle (1883–1962)
Family background: Retail sales
Education: Eureka College (1932)
Religion: Disciples of Christ
Occupation: Film actor, public official
Military service: Captain, US army reserve and army air corps, World War II
Political career: Governor of California, 1967–75
Presidential annual salary: $200,000 + $50,000 expenses
Political party: Republican
Died: 5 June 2004, Los Angeles, California

Right: Colonel Oliver North was one of those responsible for involving Reagan in the Iran-Contra scandal. He became the star witness in congressional investigations into his plan to trade arms for hostages and fund the insurrection in Nicaragua. In later years he ran for the presidency.

from Congress for 'Reaganomics', his programme of tax cuts, reductions in social services and increased defence spending. The recession of the early 1980s was the worst since the 1930s, and the budget deficit rocketed before the economy began to recover in time for the president to benefit in his 1984 re-election campaign.

The realities of 'Vietnam Syndrome', the general reluctance of Americans to support US military interventions abroad, restricted Reagan's foreign policy ambition to aggressively confront communism, seeking to reduce its international influence, particularly in Latin America. This became evident in the case of Nicaragua. He could not persuade Congress to fund a US-backed military campaign against the left-wing Sandinista government there, and this led his administration into a labyrinth of illicit activity. Money to fund the Nicaraguan Contras – the insurgents who opposed the Sandinistas – was

channelled from the proceeds of arms sales to Iran, which were made in the hope of securing the release of US hostages held in the Middle East. It was as ingenious as it was illegal. Reagan, however, was not known as the 'Teflon President' – on whom no political mud would stick – without good cause. He emerged from the scandal with his reputation battered but intact and left the White House as popular as when he first arrived there.

In October 1983, during the Lebanese Civil War, US marines stationed in Beirut as part of an international

NANCY REAGAN

She was born Nancy Robbins in New York in July 1926. Her parents divorced when she was six and in 1929 her mother married Loyal Davis, who adopted Nancy and whose name she took. She became a Hollywood actress, under contract to MGM, and in 1952 married Ronald Reagan. They had two children.

Right: Nancy Reagan was devoted to her husband, and fiercely protective of him. She was an important influence during his presidency.

Left: Relations between Margaret Thatcher, prime minister of Great Britain, and President Reagan were particularly strong.

PERESTROIKA AND GLASNOST

After Mikhail Gorbachev took over as Soviet leader in 1985, Americans became increasingly familiar with two Russian words: *perestroika* (restructuring) and *glasnost* (openness). The radical changes taking place in Soviet society altered President Reagan's perspective on the 'evil empire'. In his negotiations with Gorbachev, he became fond of quoting a Russian proverb: "*Doveriai, no proveriai*" ("Trust, but verify").

Below: Soviet troops prepare to return home at the end of the Cold War.

peacekeeping force were killed in a suicide bomb attack. Reagan withdrew US forces. In the same month, to show that the United States could still use its military power, he launched the invasion of Grenada, in response to political unrest caused by a coup that had brought a Marxist government allied to Cuba to power. It was a quick and easy victory.

Reagan believed it would be possible to make the United States immune to nuclear attack through the development of his Strategic Defense Initiative (SDI), a missile defence system known popularly as 'Star Wars'. Critics dismissed it as fantasy or worried that it would destabilize the nuclear balance of power, by which both the United States and the Soviet Union were deterred from using nuclear weapons in the knowledge that the other side had the capacity to retaliate and destroy them. When, in 1985 and 1986, Reagan finally met Mikhail Gorbachev, the last leader of the Soviet Union, in Geneva and in Reykjavik, SDI framed their discussions, and progress was made towards reductions in the levels of nuclear arms. Reagan's early anti-communist rhetoric, condemning to the 'ash-heap of history' the 'evil empire', encountered the reality of Gorbachev's aim to restructure the Soviet Union, creating a more open society.

In his declining years Reagan bore his suffering from Alzheimer's disease with characteristic grace and fortitude. When he died in 2004 he could not recall having served as one of the USA's most popular 20th-century presidents.

Below: A 1987 treaty eliminated intermediate-range nuclear missiles.

'STAR WARS'

Above: Reagan's vision, a defence system that could destroy missiles in space, alarmed those who thought it destabilized the nuclear balance of power. 'Star Wars' became a bargaining chip in negotiations between the superpowers. The Cold War came to an end after Reagan left office.

The president asked, "What if free people could live secure in the knowledge that their security did not rest upon the threat of instant US retaliation to deter a Soviet attack, that we could intercept and destroy strategic ballistic missiles before they reached our own

Below and right: Greenham Common, a US Air Force base in England became the headquarters of a women's peace movement in the 1980s. Anti-war protests became global.

soil or that of our allies?" In his address to the nation on defense and security on 23 March 1983, Ronald Reagan outlined his vision. An anti-ballistic missile shield would protect the United States from nuclear attack. Lasers and particle beams could be used to neutralize enemy missiles in space.

He challenged the scientific community "to turn their great talents now to the cause of mankind and world peace, to give us the means of rendering these nuclear weapons impotent and obsolete". The Strategic Defense Initiative Organization began to explore the problems associated with such a development. It remained a technological dream.

More significant than the practical issues was the fact that Reagan had shifted the strategic debate over nuclear weapons away from the theories of offensive deterrence, or 'mutually assured destruction', that had been developed during Eisenhower's administration. Negotiations with the Soviet Union aimed at limiting nuclear arms were now framed in a different context.

When Reagan finally talked about nuclear weapons with a communist face to face, in Geneva in November 1985, Mikhail Gorbachev came to appreciate that 'Star Wars' was based upon the US president's genuine desire to end the threat of nuclear war. In turn, Reagan saw Gorbachev's apprehension about the militarization of space – the development of weapons that could be deployed in space to be used against targets on Earth. The following year in Reykjavik, Iceland, President Reagan suggested that both sides should eliminate nuclear weapons and jointly develop SDI to safeguard against the risk of their future redeployment. Gorbachev rejected the proposal, but was convinced that Reagan would not use nuclear weapons offensively. The Russian leader was able to move forward with the defence cuts that were essential to his plans for Soviet economic reform. Reagan deserved the credit for taking a political risk that encouraged Gorbachev to become his co-star in the drama that brought the Cold War to an end.

THE IRAN–CONTRA AFFAIR

1986–1987

It was a 'neat idea' to use the proceeds of illegal arms sold to Iran, regarded by the US as a terrorist state, to fund an anti-communist insurgency in Nicaragua that Congress had refused to countenance. Colonel Oliver North, a member of President Reagan's National Security Council, did not appreciate that 'using the Ayatollah's money to support the Nicaraguan resistance' amounted to the privatization of US foreign policy. The Iran–Contra scandal broke the bounds of constitutional propriety, but Reagan survived the political firestorm when congressional committees called him to account for his actions.

In July 1985, Robert McFarlane, the national security advisor, told the president that Israel would act as an intermediary in selling arms to Iran; this would encourage Iranians who had contacts with Islamic extremist groups in Lebanon to influence the release of US hostages there. Reagan approved the plan. The first arms shipments resulted

Below: Anti-Sandinista rebels backed by the United States prepare for military action against the Nicaraguan government.

in freedom for a Presbyterian minister. The following year, North, who had been using private contributions to fund the Contras in Nicaragua, suggested to John Poindexter, McFarlane's successor, that proceeds from the arms sales could be diverted to help them in their campaign against the Nicaraguan government. In November 1986, his scheme unravelled. Justice Department investigators found the incriminating memo before his secretary, Fawn Hall, was able to shred it. Ed Meese, the attorney general, informed the

Above: A Sandinista war monument in Nicaragua commemorates the conflict and those who died.

president. Poindexter resigned. North was dismissed. In March 1987, Reagan admitted to a congressional committee: "I told the American people I did not trade arms for hostages. My heart and my best intentions still tell me that's true, but the facts and the evidence tell me it is not." The investigations concluded that he had not fulfilled his constitutional obligation to ensure "that the laws be faithfully executed".

Poindexter and North escaped jail. McFarlane, Casper Weinberger – the defense secretary later indicted for his part in the affair – and others involved received presidential pardons from George Bush, whose claim to have been "out of the loop" when arms for hostages had been discussed was later disputed. The conflict in Nicaragua continued until 1988. Violeta Chamorro, the United National Opposition candidate, defeated Daniel Ortega, the Sandinista leader, in the 1990 presidential election. In 1991, Terry Anderson, the last remaining US hostage in the Lebanon from the time of the scandal, was released.

GEORGE H. W. BUSH

1989–1993

George Bush is a member of an exclusive club: one of only four vice presidents to have been elected to succeed the presidents with whom they had served. Jefferson was re-elected but Bush, like Adams and Van Buren before him struggled to escape the shadow of a popular predecessor and failed to win a second term.

His father was Yale-educated, saw military service in World War I, was successful in business and became a Republican senator from Connecticut. Born in Massachusetts in 1924, George Bush followed in his father's footsteps: he graduated from Yale, became the youngest naval pilot in World War II and built a career in the oil industry before entering Republican politics.

Running for Congress from his adopted state of Texas, Bush served in the House of Representatives between 1967 and 1971, but lost two senate races in 1964 and 1970. President Nixon appointed him the USA's representative

Above: With the Cold War over, President Bush tried to shape a 'New World Order'.

in China, ambassador to the United Nations and chair of the Republican National Committee. He was head of the CIA during the Ford administration. Failing in his bid for the 1980 Republican presidential nomination, he became Reagan's understudy.

Famously described by *Newsweek* as a "wimp", Bush entered the 1988 presidential campaign more unpopular than any losing candidate for the previous 24 years. "Read my lips: no new taxes" was the pledge that would haunt him. He ran a negative campaign, vilifying his opponent, Michael Dukakis, and it worked. Bush won.

THE NEW WORLD ORDER

On 9 November 1989, a year and a day after George Bush had been elected president, the Berlin Wall was demolished: a symbolic event marking the end of the Cold War. Bush argued that the United States could now influence and shape a 'New World Order'. US power would guarantee international stability,

and US democracy would be an example to which other nations might aspire.

The following year the president of Iraq, Saddam Hussein, ignored Bush's message. In August, Iraq invaded Kuwait. On 11 September, addressing a joint session of Congress, Bush stated that it was his intent "to act to check that aggression". The president, who had used military force to remove Manuel Noriega from power in Panama the previous year, patiently built an international coalition with United Nations support and prepared the United States for its biggest military commitment overseas since Vietnam.

In the first test of the president's 'New World Order' US troops led a United Nations coalition in a war in the Middle East. Iraq's forces were ejected from Kuwait, which remained an independent state and a US ally in the volatile region of the Middle East. The Gulf crisis was also the president's chance to stage a final confrontation with the legacy of the nation's failure in South-east Asia. There would be, he pledged: "No more Vietnams". It was a swift and easy victory: a high-technology war with few US casualties. An exultant Bush immediately claimed that the United States had "kicked the Vietnam Syndrome once and for all". In a speech made soon after the war

---

Born: 12 June 1924, Milton, Massachusetts

Parents: Prescott (1895–1972) and Dorothy (1901–1992)

Family background: Business, public service

Education: Yale University (1948)

Religion: Episcopalian

Occupation: Businessman, public official

Military service: Lieutenant, US naval reserve, World War II

Political career: US House of Representatives, 1967–71
US ambassador to UN, 1971–2
Director of the CIA, 1976–7
Vice president, 1981–9

Presidential annual salary: $200,000 + $50,000 expenses

Political party: Republican

BARBARA BUSH

Barbara Pierce was born in 1925, in New York. She was 16 when she met George Bush. On his return from active service as a navy pilot during World War II, they married in 1945. They had six children. She was a popular first lady, and a political asset to her husband; her public approval ratings were often higher than his.

Above: George and Barbara Bush visit troops serving in the first Gulf War of 1990–1.

ended, however, the president was careful not to overreach himself and commit the United States to an overseas conflict of indeterminate length and uncertain outcome. America, he said, would not "risk being drawn into a Vietnam-style quagmire. ... Nor will we become an occupying power with US troops patrolling the streets of Baghdad". To Bush's critics, not least among neo-conservatives, his reluctance to press home his advantage demonstrated that memories of Vietnam still shaped the nation's foreign policy. In Iraq, Saddam Hussein remained in power.

After his victory in the Gulf, Bush's approval ratings stood at an all-time high. In March 1991, he had an 89 per cent approval rating. Leading Democrats were reluctant to confront an incumbent president who appeared destined to serve a second term.

Then his popularity plummeted. As the 1992 presidential election season started, Bush began to lose the political traction he had acquired from his successful foreign policy. At home, the economy worsened and memories of his broken promise not to raise taxes damaged his campaign.

The Republican party was disunited. The religious right mistrusted him. Others deserted him to support his fellow Texan, the maverick candidate Ross Perot. Bill Clinton, realizing that it was "the economy, stupid" that would decide the result, portrayed Bush as a patrician, out of touch with the concerns of ordinary Americans. The electorate agreed with him. Bush lost.

George Bush retired to the sidelines, cheering for his sons, George W., as governor of Texas, and Jeb, as governor of Florida. In 2000, he became a member of an even more exclusive club, joining John Adams as the only other former president to witness his son's election to the White House.

Below: George Bush campaigning for the presidency in 1980. Losing out to Reagan, Bush served eight years as vice president.

THE COLLAPSE OF COMMUNISM

The 'Iron Curtain' rusted from within. The Soviet Union and its various satellite governments in Eastern Europe faced an increasingly hard struggle to maintain the political disciplines of communism as their economies stumbled into stagnation. Further corrosion was caused by the tantalizing prospects of prosperity that lay just beyond the communist veil: the attractions of liberal democracy and capitalist consumerism in the West were self-evident. The dissident energy that provoked political and economic change had still to confront the state-controlled apparatus of potential repression, but in 1989, the Soviet bloc of countries began to disintegrate.

The end came quickly. On 4 June in Poland, Solidarity, the anti-communist party led by Lech Walesa, won a landslide election victory. Soviet tanks, however, remained at home. In August a human chain stretched across the Baltic States of Estonia, Latvia and Lithuania, highlighting the solidarity

Below: Crowds gather in Red Square to celebrate the failure of the attempted coup by Soviet hard-liners.

Above: Boris Yeltsin, the first president of Russia, with Mikhail Gorbachev, the last president of the Soviet Union.

of those three nations in their call for independence. In October, the Communist party in Hungary surrendered its monopoly on power. Later that same month, Erich Honecker, increasingly unpopular as East Germany's leader, was forced to resign. In Bulgaria on 11 November, the same day that the Berlin Wall was torn down, the communist leader Todor Zhivkov left office after 35 years in power. Less than two weeks later, the leadership of the Communist party in Czechoslovakia relinquished

power voluntarily. In December, Václav Havel, the dissident dramatist, became its president. In the same month, a popular revolt in Romania deposed and executed the communist dictator Nicolae Ceauşescu.

With its satellites spiralling out of its orbit, the Soviet Union now followed a similar political trajectory. In February 1990, the Communist party agreed to competitive elections taking place in each of its constituent republics. On 10 July, Boris Yeltsin took office as president of Russia. A month later he became the focus of opposition to the attempted coup against the Soviet government. Although the coup failed, it fatally undermined the political authority of Mikhail Gorbachev.

On 25 December 1991, Gorbachev resigned as president of the Soviet Union. By the end of the year, the Soviet Union itself had ceased to exist. From across the Atlantic, President George Bush and his fellow Americans watched as these last dramatic acts of the Cold War played out across Europe.

THE GULF WAR
1990–1991

On 2 August 1990, Saddam Hussein sent Iraqi forces to invade the neighbouring state of Kuwait, annexing what he claimed was Iraqi provincial territory. Others disagreed. Addressing the United Nations on 1 October 1990, President Bush compared Iraq's military aggression with the outbreak of World War I, speaking of the "still beauty of the peaceful Kuwaiti desert" being "fouled by the stench of diesel and the roar of steel tanks" as "once again … the world awoke to face the guns of August". At other times, the president likened Saddam Hussein to Hitler and Iraq's action to Germany's invasion of Poland, which provoked World War II.

After six months during which an extensive military deployment took place and efforts, encouraged by the United Nations, were made to find a diplomatic solution, US air attacks started on 16 January 1991. By then Bush was reassuring Americans that there was one war to which the conflict in the Gulf would not be comparable.

Below: On the Iraqi-Jordanian border, hundreds of displaced refugees wait in long lines for food and water from relief workers.

Announcing the commencement of 'Operation Desert Storm' he pledged that "this will not be another Vietnam".

Following five weeks of intensive air bombing, the ground war was launched on 24 February. General Norman Schwarzkopf, the US commander, borrowed a tactical manoeuvre used by Ulysses Grant at the Battle of Vicksburg. Coalition forces unleashed a 'left hook' aimed at encircling the Iraqi forces in Kuwait. Many gave up without a fight. Within four days it was over. On 28 February a ceasefire went into effect.

Above: Iraqi soldiers waving white flags surrender to coalition forces.

SADDAM REMAINS IN POWER

The objective of ejecting Iraqi forces from Kuwait had been achieved, but Saddam Hussein remained in power. Bush did not intervene militarily when the Iraqi dictator crushed the political opposition of the Kurds, concentrated in the north of the country, who sought to capitalize on Saddam's defeat by rising up against his dictatorial regime. Instead there were United Nations sanctions and the imposition of 'no-fly zones' aimed at containing Saddam's potential military threat in the region. Meanwhile inspection teams were sent to verify that Iraqi chemical, biological and nuclear weapons, which it was thought were being developed to threaten neighbouring states in the Middle East including Israel, were dismantled.

US troops remained in Saudi Arabia, offending the sensibilities of militant Islamic fundamentalists everywhere. George Bush's involvement in the turbulent world of Middle Eastern politics helped shape attitudes both within and towards the region, with repercussions that would be felt most directly after his son became president.

BILL CLINTON
1993–2001

William Blythe III was born in Hope, Arkansas, in 1946, a few months after William Jefferson Blythe, his father, died in a car accident. When he was four, his mother married Roger Clinton. While his home life was fractious because of his stepfather's alcoholism, the young Bill Clinton established a reputation as an outstanding student, a talented musician and a gregarious personality. In 1963 he shook hands with President Kennedy at the White House. A political career beckoned. In 1964 he returned to Washington to attend Georgetown University. As a student, he worked for the Senate Foreign Relations Committee, chaired by the Arkansas senator William Fulbright, by then a leading critic of the Vietnam War.

In 1965 Bill Clinton was drafted into military service. Opposed to the war, he gave up the deferment he had gained by enrolling at the University of Arkansas

Above: Bill Clinton's achievements were overshadowed by his impeachment trial following an affair with a White House intern.

Law School, gambling instead on drawing a high number in the newly introduced draft lottery, which would enable him to escape military service in Vietnam. He did. In 1970, having given up his place at Arkansas, he went to Yale Law School to complete his education. There he met Hillary Rodham.

After graduating, Clinton returned to Arkansas. He married Hillary in 1975 and their daughter, Chelsea, was born in 1980. By then, Clinton, still in his early 30s, had served as attorney general and governor of Arkansas. He failed to be re-elected at the end of his first term, but returned to office in 1982, remaining as governor for the following decade.

Presenting himself as a 'New Democrat', in 1992 Clinton won the party's presidential nomination despite being buffeted by accusations of marijuana use ("I didn't inhale"), allegations of extra-marital relationships, and suggestions that he had been a 'draft dodger'. In the presidential election he was helped by a weakened economy, divisions among Republicans, and the

quixotic campaign of the wealthy Texan, Ross Perot, which siphoned support from the Republicans, taking almost 20 per cent of the popular vote. Bill Clinton defeated Bush to become the first president of the 'baby boomer' generation. He was the youngest president to take office since John F. Kennedy.

SCANDALS AND SUCCESSES

Clinton's first two years in office mirrored his first term as state governor in being marked by political miscalculations. A campaign commitment to end discrimination against gays in the armed forces provoked a firestorm of opposition from the military. His plan for health care reform, designed by a task force chaired by Hillary (an unprecedented political role for a first lady) was complex and confusing and was rejected by Congress.

Clinton's critics were convinced that he was politically and morally corrupt. Suspicion that the Clintons had been involved in shady real-estate dealing in

Below: Bill Clinton meets John F. Kennedy at the White House in July 1963. The 16-year-old Clinton was part of the Arkansas Delegation to the American Legion Boys Nation.

Born: 19 August 1946, Hope, Arkansas

Parents: William (Blythe) (1918–1946) and Virginia (1923–1994)

Stepfather: Roger (Clinton) (1909–67)

Family background: Mother a nurse; stepfather a car dealer

Education: Georgetown University (1968), Oxford University (Rhodes Scholar 1968–70), Yale University Law School (1973)

Religion: Baptist

Occupation: Public service

Military service: None

Political career: Arkansas attorney general, 1976–8

Governor of Arkansas, 1978–80 and 1982–92

Presidential annual salary: $200,000 + $50,000 expenses

Political party: Democrat

Above: The Oklahoma bombing was the most shocking act of terrorism on US soil before the events of 11 September 2001.

Arkansas, involving the Whitewater Development Corporation which bought land to develop for vacation homes, was compounded after Clinton's personal lawyer, Vince Foster, committed suicide. In January 1994 Robert Fiske was appointed as a 'special prosecutor' to investigate.

In the 1994 mid-term elections, the Republicans won control of both houses of Congress. The new Speaker, Newt Gingrich, rapidly established

HILLARY CLINTON

Born in Chicago in October 1947, Hillary Rodham graduated from Wellesley College, then went to Yale Law School, where she met Bill Clinton. They married in 1975. She stood by her husband during the scandals that rocked his presidency. In January 2007 she announced her candidacy for the 2008 Democrat presidential nomination, in a bid to return to the White House as the first woman to be elected president of the United States.

himself as the focus of opposition to the president. The following year Congress and the president battled over plans to balance the federal budget, and their refusal to compromise led to a delay in agreeing the level of federal expenditure in time to prevent a partial shutdown of the government, which could no longer pay its employees. Among those who continued to work in the White House were the unpaid political interns, one of whom was Monica Lewinsky.

Showing his trademark resilience, Clinton recovered from political setbacks to become the first Democrat to be re-elected president since Franklin Roosevelt. Clinton's political abilities were matched by his lack of moral sensibility. During his second term, rumours about Clinton and Lewinsky first appeared on the internet. It was Republican outrage at his personal behaviour in prevaricating about their affair, and subsequently being forced to acknowledge it, that led to an unsuccessful attempt to impeach him.

He extended free trade through the North American Free Trade Agreement (NAFTA), the economy hummed along and the federal budget deficit diminished. Abroad, Clinton extended

NAFTA

The North American Free Trade Agreement (NAFTA) came into effect on 1 January 1994. It aimed to eliminate obstacles to trade and investment between the United States, Canada and Mexico. While its American critics remain suspicious of its impact upon employment, particularly in manufacturing industries, its supporters point to the economic growth and rising living standards that have resulted from the free-market economy in North America.

diplomatic recognition to Vietnam. He was instrumental in developing Northern Ireland's peace process, and after sanctioning military intervention in the Balkans he brokered a peace accord between Bosnia, Serbia and Croatia. Iraq continued to be a problem, and terrorism, notably the 1995 bombing in Oklahoma City, remained a threat.

Below: A politically committed first lady, in November 2000, Hillary Clinton was elected to the Senate from New York.

Above: Senate Republicans could not muster enough votes for the impeachment of Clinton to be successful.

THE IMPEACHMENT TRIAL

When radical Republicans focused their attention on holding the president to account for his standards of behaviour in the White House, and when Hillary Clinton suggested there was a vast right-wing conspiracy against her husband, they defined a contemporary fault line in US political debate. Since Nixon's conduct during Watergate, the issue of morality in US public life had been a consistent concern. Throughout his presidency, Clinton's moral and political integrity had been under attack, particularly from those who drew support from the increasingly vocal fundamentalist wing of the Republican party.

In August 1994, special prosecutor Robert Fiske was replaced by Kenneth Starr, a Republican. Meanwhile, an Arkansas state employee, Paula Jones, brought a lawsuit against Clinton, alleging that he had sexually harassed her while he was governor. The stage was set for the drama of impeachment. All that remained was to cast the starring role of a White House intern who had had an affair with the president: Monica Lewinsky.

By the time of Clinton's re-election in 1996, Starr had not been able to find significant evidence of misconduct in the Whitewater affair, the original remit of his investigation. The following year, Lewinsky revealed details of her relationship with Clinton to Linda Tripp, a former White House employee then working at the Pentagon. After Lewinsky denied the affair in an affidavit given to Paula Jones's lawyers, Tripp contacted Starr, who was then able to pursue a new line of enquiry: possible obstruction of justice and perjury orchestrated by the president.

When the House Judiciary Committee received his report it gave them the ammunition they needed to detonate the impeachment process.

The mathematics were simple. A two-thirds majority in the Senate was required to vote in favour of the charges brought by the House of Representatives. There were 45 Democrat senators. Whereas the impeachment trial of President Andrew Johnson had hung in the balance, it was widely acknowledged that Bill Clinton's opponents did not have the necessary support to convict him. The proceedings that took place in Congress during 1998 were a political entertainment in which the eventual outcome was predictable. Clinton survived with his reputation tarnished but his popularity undimmed.

Clinton's election had symbolized a generational change in US politics. Reactions to his personal conduct demonstrated that the nation's fragmented cultural and countercultural values coexisted in uneasy tension. Despite this, on leaving office, Bill Clinton was characteristically optimistic about the USA's future prospects. As he put it: "I still believe in a place called Hope."

Below: Monica Lewinsky (in blue) runs the media gauntlet following the revelation of her affair with the president.

THE INVENTION OF THE INTERNET

When *Newsweek* decided not to publish allegations of the relationship between Bill Clinton and Monica Lewinsky, the story was initially revealed on Matt Drudge's website. During the 1990s, the internet became a new and powerful medium of political communication. It was potentially democratic, allowing anyone to present their political views unmediated and unvarnished to a national and international audience.

On 11 September 1998, when Kenneth Starr's report containing details of the affair was first made available to anyone who had access to the internet, the website on which it had been posted received more than three million hits per hour. The internet, like the printing press, radio and television before it, ushered in a communications revolution. Politicians, including the president of the United States, have to adapt to a world where more and more people are part of the online network.

The way that the internet shapes the modern world has been the product of the interface between innovative technologies that have made personal computers an essential feature of everyday life. At the turn of the 21st century there were more than 45 million Americans subscribing to the internet. Bill Gates, the co-founder of Microsoft, which had developed the dominant operating system facilitating its use, had become the richest person on the planet.

For politicians, the internet has become an indispensable means of advertising themselves to potential voters. The White House website (www.whitehouse.gov) currently provides an official account of the public lives of the president, the first lady, the vice president and his wife. The impact of the internet has been felt particularly during elections, when it has provided candidates with innovative ways to

reach potential supporters and, just as importantly, more effective ways to raise money for campaigns.

The internet is potentially an ideal medium for democratic debate, allowing anyone to voice their opinions on the issues about which they are concerned. But issues remain. Are there limits to be imposed on freedom of speech, or on the actions of those who seek to influence others to embrace their

Left: Tim Berners Lee, changed the face of communications throughout the world when he developed the internet.

particular ideas, attitudes or prejudices? How trustworthy is the information available on individual websites?

In 1999, Al Gore, the then vice president, suggested that as a senator from Tennessee he "took the initiative in creating the internet", meaning that he promoted the use of the new technology. Unfortunately, his words as he prepared to run for the White House were easily altered by his opponents. They claimed that he said that he had 'invented' it: an inaccurate quotation that spread rapidly through cyberspace, making him the object of widespread ridicule. The internet has the potential to shape the popular images of aspiring presidents in new and possibly unanticipated ways.

Below: Mass access to the internet led to a communications revolution, allowing politicians greater opportunities to reach potential supporters and influence voters.

THE PRESIDENTIAL ELECTION

2000

The first presidential election of the 21st century was decided not by the American people but by the Supreme Court. George W. Bush, son of the former president, won the White House through the intervention of judges who had been nominated either by his father or by Ronald Reagan, after an election in which disputed votes in Florida, governed by his brother, were critical to the outcome.

The electoral college seemed a benign constitutional anachronism. It had worked throughout the 20th century. It was the first election of the new millennium that focused attention on the institution, which had, except on three previous occasions, avoided the political spotlight. Thomas Jefferson in 1800 and John Quincy Adams in 1824 had been elected by the House of Representatives. Rutherford Hayes had been awarded the White House in 1888 by an electoral commission composed of members of Congress and the Supreme Court. In 2000, it would be the Supreme Court alone that effectively decided the result.

Left: George Bush and Al Gore contested one of the most controversial elections in presidential history.

Above: The 2000 presidential election result was subject to intense scrutiny.

Twelve years previously George H. W. Bush, then vice president, had defeated a state governor, Michael Dukakis, to become chief executive. Now George W. Bush, governor of Texas, challenged the incumbent vice president, Al Gore. The outcome was predicted to be close. Gore, who had served Clinton loyally, benefited from the economic prosperity that had marked the Democrats' eight years in the White House, but found it difficult to distance himself from the charges of corruption, in his case political rather than moral, that bedevilled the administration. Bush, who had won the nomination for his party after a hard-fought battle against his principal rival, Senator John McCain, pledged to restore "honor and dignity" to the White House, but his apparent lack of interest in the politics of the wider world led his detractors to doubt his presidential credentials.

On election night, the television networks correctly predicted that the key to victory would lie with the result in Florida. In their competition to be the first to report the outcome, the commentators agreed early in the evening that Bush had carried the state. They were wrong. After the results elsewhere in the country had been called, Gore telephoned Bush to concede defeat. Shortly afterwards, it became apparent that the Florida vote was in fact too close to call. The two candidates spoke again. Gore withdrew his concession.

FLORIDA

Florida state law required a recount. Then voting irregularities emerged. The ballot papers took the form of punch cards designed to be counted mechanically, and Americans became used to discussing the intricacies of 'butterfly ballots' and 'chads' that could be 'hanging', 'dimpled' or 'pregnant'. Arguments developed over how many votes were valid. The lawyers moved in. Courtroom battles decided to allow manual recounts and set deadlines for

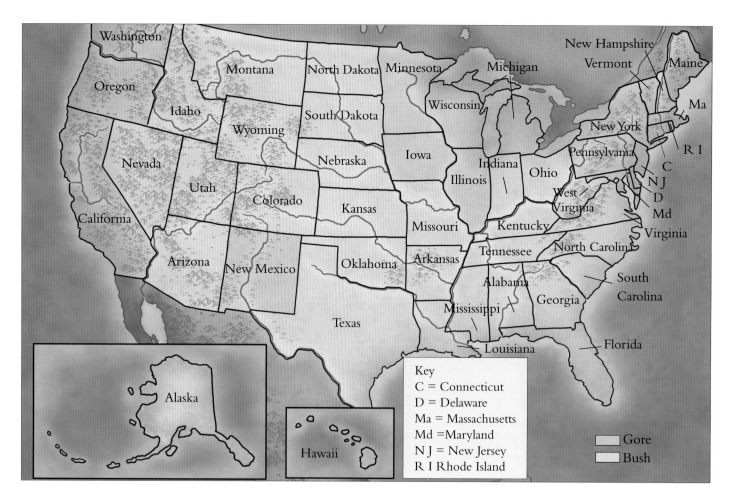

Above: The result of the presidential election of 2000 was determined by the votes of one state, Florida.

their completion. On 26 November, 19 days after the election, Katherine Harris, Florida's secretary of state, certified the Florida result: Bush had won by 537 votes, out of the almost six million that had been cast. Gore disagreed.

SUPREME COURT DECISION

The legal arguments and the recounting continued while the Florida State Legislature met to consider how to select its electors in the event that the dispute remained unresolved. The Republican majority, supported by Governor Jeb Bush, would have been expected to endorse those pledged to support their party's candidate. It proved unnecessary when the Supreme Court delivered its verdict. On 12 December, by a 5–4 vote, it decided that the recounts were unconstitutional as they were not being conducted according to

a consistent standard in different Florida counties. They were stopped. The certification of Florida's result was endorsed. Bush had gained the critical one-vote majority he needed in the electoral college to win the election.

Overall, Gore had won the national popular vote but, like Samuel Tilden before him, he had lost where the outcome was decided: the electoral college had 'misfired'. Effectively, the Supreme Court had selected the president. The five judges who agreed the majority decision had been nominated by Republican presidents. Of the two justices appointed during his father's presidency, one, Clarence Thomas, sided with Bush. The other, David Souter, did not.

By involving itself in the partisan world normally inhabited by the executive and the legislature, the Court's reputation for independence was diminished. As one of those who dissented from its verdict, Justice John Paul Stevens, put it: "Although we may never

know with complete certainty the identity of the winner of this year's presidential election, the identity of the loser is perfectly clear. It is the Nation's confidence in the judge as an impartial guardian of the rule of law." On 20 January 2001, George W. Bush was inaugurated as the 43rd president.

BUTTERFLY BALLOTS AND CHADS

The 'butterfly ballot', with the names of the candidates' names down both sides separated by punch holes in the centre, was a design that potentially confused voters. 'Chads' are the paper waste made when a machine punches a hole in paper. A 'hanging' chad might have one corner still attached to the ballot; 'pregnant' and 'dimpled' chads were still fixed firmly to the ballot but with varying signs of indentation, possibly indicating an intention to vote for a particular candidate.

GEORGE W. BUSH
2001–2009

The defining moment of George Bush's presidency came on 11 September 2001, when terrorist attacks on the United States changed the face of domestic and international politics. His term in office was shaped by his reaction to the events of that single day. The attacks, which destroyed the twin towers of the World Trade Center in New York City, damaged the Pentagon, and threatened intended targets in Washington DC, led to his declaration of a 'war on terror'. Military action followed in Afghanistan. Then came Iraq. When the weapons of mass destruction that had provided the pretext for an invasion of Iraq proved elusive, the president's credibility crumbled. Saddam Hussein's regime in Iraq was toppled, but US troops were drawn into a prolonged conflict that eroded Bush's popularity. As his term in office entered its final months, his approval ratings were among the lowest ever recorded.

Born in 1946 and brought up in Texas, George W. Bush's journey into politics was the product of family expectation and tradition. He was not

Above: Contemporary approval ratings for Bush have been some of the highest and lowest ever recorded for a US president.

an outstanding student at Yale, although he enjoyed the social life of his fraternity. Service in the Texas Air National Guard, where he learned to fly, meant that he did not go to Vietnam. After graduating from Harvard Business School in 1975, he returned to Texas and a career in the oil industry.

At the age of 40, Bush gave up alcohol for sobriety. Encouraged by the Reverend Billy Graham, he dedicated himself to a life that would make him the most overtly religious occupant of the White House since Jimmy Carter. His public profile in his home state was raised by his part-ownership of the Texas Rangers baseball team. In 1994, helped by Karl Rove, his principal political strategist, he ran for governor of Texas. His landslide re-election four years later was followed in 2000 by his successful campaign for the Republican presidential nomination.

After the Supreme Court had settled the arguments and lawsuits that swirled around the Florida recounts, George W. Bush, like John Quincy Adams before

him, followed in his father's footsteps as he became the first president to take office in the 21st century.

11 SEPTEMBER 2001

After seven months in the White House, during which US foreign policy became more unilateralist – symbolized by Bush's refusal to sign the Kyoto Protocol on International Climate Change – his lack of popularity abroad was mirrored by low approval ratings at home. His vice president, Dick Cheney, who had served Bush's father as defense secretary during the 1991 Gulf War, was widely believed to be the driving force behind the administration's policies.

Then came 11 September. It gave Bush the opportunity to reinvigorate his presidency. His reaction, declaring a 'war on terror', and subsequently announcing the 'Bush Doctrine' in justification of pre-emptive military action to counter perceived threats to national security, provoked domestic opposition

Below: Pope John Paul II and President George W. Bush at the papal summer residence in July 2001.

Born: 6 July 1946, New Haven, Connecticut
Parents: George (b. 1924) and Barbara (b.1925)
Family background: Business, public service
Education: Yale University (1968), Harvard Business School (1975)
Religion: Methodist
Occupation: Business
Military service: First lieutenant, Alabama air national guard
Political career: Governor of Texas, 1995–2000
Presidential annual salary: $400,000 + $50,000 expenses
Political party: Republican

Above: Saddam Hussein's statue is toppled. Televised worldwide, this event symbolized the end of his regime, but the continuing insurgency has involved the United States in a protracted war with Iraq.

Above: The military campaigns in President Bush's 'war on terror' following the attacks of 11 September 2001 will remain his most controversial legacy.

and drained the reservoir of overseas sympathy in the aftermath of the terrorist attacks.

By the end of the year, the Taliban regime in Afghanistan, which had provided a base for Osama Bin Laden and Al Qaeda training camps, had been overthrown by a US-led coalition operating with United Nations approval. In his 2002 State of the Union address, Bush proceeded to identify an 'Axis of Evil' – Iraq, Iran and North Korea – which he suggested represented further threats to US security.

The next phase of the 'war on terror' fractured relations between the United States and the international community, with the notable exception of the United Kingdom. In 2003 Bush's dwindling 'coalition of the willing' invaded Iraq. Saddam Hussein was overthrown, and US troops remained in a hostile country where the political, economic and social infrastructure had been destroyed and there was no immediate prospect of its reconstruction. The war continued. Despite the controversy surrounding his actions, Bush won re-election in 2004. His second term was soon blown off course by the administration's inept reaction to the devastation caused when, in August 2005, Hurricane Katrina destroyed New Orleans. In the following year's mid-term elections, the Democrats regained control of Congress, and the president's popularity reached its lowest ebb. George W. Bush ensured that the presidency remains the focus of national attention and that future occupants of the White House will have to confront complex and politically divisive issues of war and peace. Barack Obama, his Democratic successor, won the 2008 election, as the aftershocks of Bush's controversial eight years in the White House continued to shape the future of United States politics.

LAURA BUSH

Laura Welch was born in Texas in 1946. After graduating from Southern Methodist University in Dallas she became a schoolteacher. On gaining a Masters degree she worked as a school librarian. In 1977, she married George W. Bush. Their twin daughters, Jenna and Barbara, were born four years later. She is credited with playing an influential part in his decision to stop drinking in 1986. Uncomfortable in the political spotlight, as first lady she emulated her mother-in-law, Barbara Bush, and concentrated on supporting her husband and promoting education and women's health.

AL QAEDA

Al Qaeda, translated as 'the base', is a Sunni Muslim fundamentalist group, led by Osama Bin Laden, that grew out of the religious and political conflict in Afghanistan in the 1980s. After the 1991 Gulf War, the continuing presence of US troops in Saudi Arabia became a focus of its hostility towards the United States, ultimately leading to its organization of the 11 September attacks and prompting President Bush's 'war on terror'. Among the group's aims are an end to foreign influence in Muslim countries and the establishment of a new caliphate.

9/11/2001

The images are seared into the USA's historical memory. On the morning of 11 September 2001, television cameras recorded events as first American Airlines flight 11, which had left Boston en route to Los Angeles, and then United Airlines flight 175, scheduled to make the same journey, exploded into each of the twin towers of the World Trade Center in New York City. Shortly after those initial impacts, American Airlines flight 77 from Washington DC to Los Angeles slammed into the Pentagon. A fourth plane, United Airlines flight 93, which had been delayed taking off from Newark on its way to San Francisco, was the last of the hijacked airliners to crash: it came down in a rural area of south-west Pennsylvania without reaching its presumed target in the nation's capital. Nearly 3,000 people lost their lives. It was the worst terrorist atrocity that had ever been perpetrated on US soil.

President Bush, who was in Florida, made a brief announcement: "We have had a national tragedy. Two aeroplanes have crashed into the World Trade Center in an apparent terrorist attack on our country." Less than 20 minutes

after he had spoken, airports were closed and commercial flights suspended across the country. As the full scale of the attacks emerged, the president flew first to Louisiana, where he vowed to "hunt down and punish those responsible for these cowardly acts", then to Nebraska, before returning to Washington. That evening, in a nationwide address, he proclaimed that the United States would "make no distinction between the terrorists who committed these acts and those who harbor them".

In New York, it was the mayor, Rudolph Giuliani, who took control of the situation in the hours following the attacks. The nation looked to its president to provide leadership. On 13 September, in a televised conference call with Giuliani and George Pataki, the governor of New York, Bush, who had initially not planned to visit New York that week, announced that he would fly to the city the following afternoon after attending a service at Washington National Cathedral. In his address to a congregation there that included three former presidents – his father, Jimmy Carter and Bill Clinton – Bush said: "This conflict has begun on the timing

and terms of others. It will end in a way, and at an hour, of our choosing." The service ended with the singing of 'The Battle Hymn of the Republic'.

Later, in New York, he improvised the most effective three sentences of his presidency. Standing on a battered fire truck rescued from the wreckage of the collapsed buildings, Bush struggled to make himself heard as he spoke through a bullhorn. Someone in the crowd complained of being unable to hear him. The president, with his arm around the shoulders of a firefighter, responded: "I can hear you. The rest of the world hears you. And the people who knocked these buildings down will hear from all of us soon."

It was an image of defiance and resolve that was rapidly translated into substance. Osama Bin Laden, whose Al Qaeda terrorist network was immediately suspected of planning and executing the attacks, was held responsible: less than a week after 9/11, the president had announced that he was 'Wanted, Dead or Alive'. His sanctuary in Afghanistan would be the first target in the 'war on terror'.

As investigations continued into how the 19 hijackers had been allowed to enter the United States and take commercial flight training courses, national security became a major concern. In October, Congress passed the Patriot Act, increasing government powers to fight terrorism, which led to concerns that civil liberties were threatened. After the war in Afghanistan, suspected terrorists were taken to Guantanamo Bay, the US military facility in Cuba, where they were detained without trial. Osama Bin Laden's precise whereabouts remained unknown.

Left: The twin towers ablaze in New York. In his diary that night Bush recorded that "The Pearl Harbor of the 21st century took place today."

THE IRAQ WAR
2003

President Bush's 'war on terror' involved the United States in its most protracted overseas military action since Vietnam. From the end of 2001 onwards, the inconclusive conflict in Afghanistan was relegated to a sideshow as the administration turned its attention towards Iraq.

Iraq was the 'unfinished business' left over from the Gulf War of 1991. Its head of state, Saddam Hussein, was a dictatorial leader who defied the UN sanctions regime that tried to curb his abuse of power, who still had the potential to threaten neighbouring states in the Middle East and who, it was claimed, might also be stockpiling weapons of mass destruction. The Bush administration held him responsible for encouraging international terrorism, even though they could not establish that he had any obvious links with groups such as Al Qaeda. In January 2002, Iraq became a charter member of President Bush's so-called 'Axis of Evil'.

Five months later, in his speech at West Point, the president revealed that the ground was being prepared. In formulating the 'Bush Doctrine', he

Below: Saddam Hussein was deposed, captured and tried in Iraq.

Above: The US-led 'coalition of the willing' invaded Iraq, but found no weapons of mass destruction there.

warned that: "The gravest danger to freedom lies at the perilous crossroads of radicalism and technology. When the spread of chemical and biological and nuclear weapons, along with ballistic missile technology, occurs, even weak states and small groups could attain a catastrophic power to strike great nations. Our enemies ... have been caught seeking these terrible weapons ... Unbalanced dictators with weapons of mass destruction can deliver those weapons on missiles or secretly provide them to terrorist allies." He concluded that the United States needed "to be ready for pre-emptive action when necessary to defend our liberty".

The CIA supplied the intelligence. In December 2002, its then director, George Tenet, told the president that it was a "slam dunk case" that Saddam had concealed weapons of mass destruction. The UN weapons inspectors, who had resumed their work the previous month, would not be so confident about their existence.

The president was convinced, however, and on 28 January 2003, in his State of the Union address, he made a commitment: "If Saddam Hussein does not fully disarm, for the safety of our people and for the peace of the world,

we will lead a coalition to disarm him." The United States claimed that 40 nations were represented in a 'coalition of the willing' that supported action against Iraq, although only four – Britain, Poland, Denmark and Australia – contributed troops to the invasion force.

HOSTILITIES BEGIN

The war began on 20 March and Saddam's government rapidly collapsed. When US troops occupied Baghdad he was nowhere to be found. It soon became apparent that Saddam had bluffed. No weapons of mass destruction were discovered. On 13 December the former dictator was discovered, hiding underground in Tikrit. By then, Iraq was spiralling into violent conflict between militant Sunni and Shi'ite Muslims and Kurdish nationals, with the Americans and their coalition allies, among whom the British remained prominent, struggling to impose order. Optimism that, freed from dictatorship, Iraq would develop into a model liberal democracy were profoundly misplaced.

At the end of April 2004, the United States surrendered most of its remaining moral high ground in the court of world opinion when images of prisoner abuse at Abu Ghraib prison, Baghdad, were released. In June, political sovereignty was transferred back to Iraq, a country in which internal security had now collapsed into a maelstrom of militia rivalries, hostage taking and suicide bombings.

Saddam Hussein was executed on 30 December 2006, having been found guilty by an Iraqi court of crimes against humanity. His country's ordeal continued. George W. Bush's final months in the White House offered scant prospect of influencing the contemporary conclusion that his mission in Iraq remained unaccomplished. History's verdict remains to be drawn.

HURRICANE KATRINA
2005

Thomas Jefferson acquired New Orleans through the Louisiana Purchase in 1803. It was founded in 1718 by the French Mississippi Company, and was among America's oldest cities. Andrew Jackson established his military reputation there. In 1988 it hosted the Republican national convention that nominated George H. W. Bush for the presidency. Famous as the birthplace of jazz, for its Mardi Gras and its French Quarter, about half of New Orleans was built below sea level, and it is surrounded by water: the Mississippi River, Lake Pontchartrain and a system of slow-moving streams known as bayous.

On Monday 29 August 2005, the city became part of the lake. As Hurricane Katrina cut a swathe across Louisiana, Mississippi and Alabama, in New Orleans the levees that had been its defence against flooding were breached. As the waters continued to rise, a humanitarian disaster threatened in the wake of the environmental devastation.

The president was on vacation at his ranch in Texas. On the day before the hurricane's landfall, George W. Bush

Below: The impact of the hurricane was most severely felt in New Orleans, where the loss of life was greatest.

spoke with Mike Brown, who was in charge of the Federal Emergency Management Agency (FEMA), the body responsible for responding to natural disasters. Bush told reporters: "We will do everything in our power to help the people in the communities affected by this storm."

As the storm's full impact became clear, he returned to Washington, flying over New Orleans on his way back to the White House. On the ground, conditions were deteriorating in the city's Superdome, where refugees from the

Above: Hurricane Katrina was one of America's worst natural disasters, displacing people and ruining lives.

storm had been left stranded in its aftermath. In the city, law and order temporarily broke down as widespread looting took place.

Amid criticism that his administration was offering insufficient help, Bush toured the stricken area on Friday 2 September and expressed his confidence in FEMA's response to the disaster: "Brownie, you're doing a heck of a job." A week later Brown was dismissed from his job of managing the relief effort. He later resigned as FEMA's head.

It was those who had least who were the most dispossessed: those with cars left the city; the poor, elderly and homeless were left stranded. Hurricane Katrina exposed the disparities in US society between the rich and the poor, and between the white and black populations of the South. George W. Bush, beleaguered by the Iraq War, found his leadership once more in the spotlight of media attention, compounding the political problems caused by his controversial foreign policy.

BARACK OBAMA

2009–

On November 4th 2008, Barack Obama was elected president, the culmination of a remarkable personal and political odyssey. He was born in Honolulu, Hawaii, in 1961. His mother, Ann Dunham, was from Kansas, and his father, for whom he was named, was from Kenya. Their mixed-race marriage did not endure after Barack senior left to study at Harvard, and then returned to Africa. Obama's mother remarried and in 1967 took her young son to live in Jakarta, but after four years there, he returned to Hawaii to be brought up by his maternal grandparents.

In 1983 he graduated from Columbia University, in New York, and two years later moved to Chicago to be an organizer among the city's deprived and predominantly African-American South Side community. In 1988 he went to Harvard Law School, gaining national attention as the first black president of its law review. Returning to Chicago in 1991, he began teaching at the University of Chicago Law School.

The following year he married Michelle Robinson. In 1995 his autobiographical account of his search for identity, *Dreams from My Father* was published, and a year later Obama won election to the Illinois State Senate.

In 2004, now seeking election to the federal Senate, Obama's inspirational rhetoric was demonstrated in his keynote address at the Democratic National Convention, which nominated John Kerry for president. He won his Senate contest and just three years later entered the race for the Democratic Party presidential nomination, galvanizing his supporters in an insurgent primary campaign against the front-runner and heir apparent, Hillary Clinton. Obama's powerful message of generational and political change brought victory over the Republican candidate, John McCain,

Below: Barack Obama is the first African-American president in US history, and also one of the youngest presidents ever to take office.

in a hard fought, often bitter and increasingly negative election contest. During the campaign the American economy nearly collapsed and the wars in Afghanistan and Iraq rumbled on. Obama faces formidable domestic and international challenges as president, but his success affirmed to many not only the enduring promise of American life, but also 'the audacity of hope', as expressed in the title of the book he published in 2006, which, soon afterwards, would become the manifesto for his presidential ambition.

MICHELLE OBAMA

Michelle Robinson was born in 1964 and grew up on the South Side of Chicago. A graduate of Princeton and Harvard Law School, and a successful career woman, she married Barack Obama in 1992. They have two daughters, Malia and Sasha, the youngest children to live in the White House since Amy Carter, 32 years ago.

Born: 4 August 1961, Honolulu, Hawaii
Parents: Ann (1942–95) and Barack (1936–82)
Family background: Mother: anthropologist, father: public service
Education: Columbia University (1983)
Harvard Law School (1991)
Religion: United Church of Christ
Occupation: Public Service, Academic
Military service: none
Political career: Illinois State Senate (1996–2004)
US Senate (2004–08)
Presidential annual salary: $400,000 + $50,000 expenses
Political party: Democrat

INDEX